EX
LIBRIS
WESTFIELD
COLLEGE

CAMBRIDGE STUDIES
IN
MEDIEVAL LIFE AND THOUGHT

Edited by G. G. COULTON, Litt.D., Hon. D.Litt., Hon. LL.D., F.B.A.
Fellow of St John's College, Cambridge, Honorary Fellow of St Catharine's College, University Lecturer in English

CHURCH LIFE IN ENGLAND UNDER EDWARD III

LONDON
Cambridge University Press
FETTER LANE

NEW YORK · TORONTO
BOMBAY · CALCUTTA · MADRAS
Macmillan

TOKYO
Maruzen Company Ltd

PRINTED IN GREAT BRITAIN

STUDIES IN CHURCH LIFE IN ENGLAND UNDER EDWARD III

BY

K. L. WOOD-LEGH

M.A. McGill, B.Litt. Oxon., Ph.D. Cantab.

CAMBRIDGE
AT THE UNIVERSITY PRESS
1934

TO
MY UNCLE
W. E. STEVENSON

GENERAL PREFACE

THERE is only too much truth in the frequent complaint that history, as compared with the physical sciences, is neglected by the modern public. But historians have the remedy in their own hands; choosing problems of equal importance to those of the scientist, and treating them with equal accuracy, they will command equal attention. Those who insist that the proportion of accurately ascertainable facts is smaller in history, and therefore the room for speculation wider, do not thereby establish any essential distinction between truth-seeking in history and truth-seeking in chemistry. The historian, whatever be his subject, is as definitely bound as the chemist "to proclaim certainties as certain, falsehoods as false, and uncertainties as dubious". Those are the words, not of a modern scientist, but of the seventeenth century monk, Jean Mabillon; they sum up his literary profession of faith. Men will follow us in history as implicitly as they follow the chemist, if only we will form the chemist's habit of marking clearly where our facts end and our inferences begin. Then the public, so far from discouraging our speculations, will most heartily encourage them; for the most positive man of science is always grateful to anyone who, by putting forward a working theory, stimulates further discussion.

The present series, therefore, appeals directly to that craving for clearer facts which has been bred in these times of storm and stress. No care can save us altogether from error; but for our own sake and the public's we have elected to adopt a safeguard dictated by ordinary business common-sense. Whatever errors of fact are pointed out by reviewers or correspondents shall be publicly corrected with the least possible delay. After a year of publication, all copies shall be provided with such an erratum-slip without waiting for the chance of a second edition; and each fresh volume in this series shall contain a full list of the errata noted in its immediate predecessor. After the lapse of a year from the first publication of any volume, and at any time during the ensuing twelve months, any possessor of that volume who will send a stamped and addressed envelope to the Cambridge University Press, Fetter Lane, Fleet Street, London, E.C. 4, shall receive, in due course, a free copy of the *errata* in that volume. Thus, with the help of our critics, we may reasonably hope to put forward these monographs as roughly representing the most accurate information obtainable under present conditions. Our facts being thus secured, the reader will judge our inferences on their own merits; and something will have been done to dissipate that cloud of suspicion which hangs over too many important chapters in the social and religious history of the Middle Ages.

G. G. C.

Oct. 1922

INTRODUCTION

THE value of the records preserved by the English Chancery as sources from which many aspects of medieval history may be studied has long been recognized. Ever since the time when Prynne began to disinter them from the cobwebs and filth in which they were then lying, they have yielded new treasures to each successive generation of historians and antiquaries. Yet, although the work of searching these records has been going on for nearly three centuries, their store of information is far from exhausted.

That this is so must be attributed largely to the fact that the amount of material which the records contain is so vast that even after a lifetime of study one could hope to be familiar with only a comparatively small proportion of the existing documents. Now, however, much of the practical difficulty of consulting these records has been removed by the publication of calendars of several important series of rolls, which give in concise English form the substance of each document. The calendars are, of course, not free from errors in translation, and from time to time, also, they omit details which would be of some interest. But, as a rule, they are sufficiently reliable to be used confidently without recourse to the originals, and thus the possibilities of discovering what the chancery records contain, and of examining them from new points of view, have been enormously increased.

It was natural that the first persons to make full use of the calendars should have been the constitutional and administrative historians, but these records are often hardly less important to the student of ecclesiastical history. That they were of some importance for the history of the church has, indeed, long been recognized. For even before the calendars began to be published those who were concerned with this subject were in the habit of consulting the chancery records. Their methods of employing these sources, however, have not been altogether satisfactory. The majority of those who have dealt with the history of the English church as a whole have used the chancery records only as secondary sources, which might from time to time add something to what could be learned from the records which the church itself has left, but which merited only a very superficial examination. In the writing of local history the chancery records have been used to greater advantage, and the accounts of many individual religious houses admirably combine the information derived from ecclesiastical and lay sources, showing, incidentally, how essential are both to an understanding of the church's history. But even from these works we do not learn the full value of the chancery documents, for many of the most interesting items to which they direct our attention lose much of their significance when considered from a purely local point of view and apart from similar items relating to other places.

My first intimate knowledge of the chancery records was acquired when I was investigating some aspects of our early parliamentary history. While searching the Calendars of Patent, Close and Fine Rolls, for details concerning the knights of the shire, I observed with surprise how large a proportion of the items in the calendars related in some way to the affairs of the church. There were licences for alienations in mortmain, commissions for the visitation of hospitals in the king's gift, appointments of custodians for financially embarrassed monasteries, orders for the arrest of apostate monks, presentations to livings of the king's patronage, recognizances of debts in which clerics were concerned either as borrowers or lenders, pardons to monks and secular clerks for all kinds of offences and misdemeanours, commissions to investigate charges of violence made sometimes by and sometimes against members of the clerical order, and many other matters affecting the daily lives of the medieval clergy and their relations with their lay neighbours. Such a wealth of detail seemed likely to repay careful study, and it seemed to me, therefore, that much might be gained if an examination of the chancery records or of some important series of them could be undertaken with a view to discovering what they could add to our knowledge of the medieval church in England, and the present work is an attempt to carry out this plan.

I have chosen as the period of my study the reign of Edward III, partly because the possibility of discovering some evidence as to the effects of the Black Death made it appear to the researcher a particularly promising period, but mainly because it is a period of suitable length, and one for which we have complete calendars of most of the important chancery rolls.

The study has been based mainly on the Calendar of the Patent Rolls, which of all the chancery enrolments appeared to be the richest source of ecclesiastical items, and which I have endeavoured to examine, not with preconceived notions of what I should find, but rather in the spirit of an explorer desirous of discovering what the new tract contained.

My first task was therefore to read through the entire series of volumes of the Calendar of Patent Rolls for the reign of Edward III, endeavouring to note all the items that concerned the church. Gradually it became apparent that although almost every aspect of the life of the church was occasionally mentioned, there were many matters to which reference was made only rarely and by chance, while other matters in which the interests of the state were involved constantly occupied the attention of the chancery and were regularly enrolled. To discuss all the evidence with regard to the church which the Patent Rolls of this period contain would require a work far exceeding the length prescribed for the present study, and since a selection of material was necessary it seemed best to concentrate attention on those subjects concerning which the Patent Rolls gave the fullest information. Accordingly five topics on which the Patent Rolls are particularly instructive have been chosen, and each has been made the subject of a separate essay. But although the basis of each study has of course been the evidence derived from the Patent Rolls, I have, in order to show this evidence in its true perspective, and often indeed to make it at all comprehensible, made constant use of material drawn from other sources; these have included the Calendars of Close and Fine Rolls, and of Miscellaneous Inquisitions, the Calendars of Papal Letters and Petitions, and the printed Episcopal Registers and Borough Records.

Two important topics which anyone familiar with the Patent Rolls might expect to find discussed in these essays have been omitted as a consequence of the work already done by other investigators. One of these is the royal patronage, for a study of which the Patent Rolls with their records of the presentations to livings in the king's gift provide ample material, but it was thought that such a study could add little to what can be learned from the articles on "The Patronage of Edward I" by Dr R. A. R. Hartridge, and on "Papal Provisions and Royal Rights of Patronage" by Miss A. Deeley. Similarly the Alien Priories have not found a place among these studies because the material concerning them has been satisfactorily examined in Mr C. W. New's monograph.

With these exceptions, I believe that the principal subjects that can profitably be studied with the Patent Rolls as a main source have been dealt with in the following pages. It was inevitable that such a work should appear somewhat lacking in unity, since the chapters of which it is composed are held together mainly by the fact that they are all based on the same source and all concern the church. It is hoped, however, that this will not be considered a serious defect and that the present work may be of some value both by adding to our knowledge of the life of the church during a particular period, and by illustrating the importance of the chancery enrolments to the student of ecclesiastical history.

Important parts of the chapters on Chantries and on the appropriation of Parish Churches have already been published as articles in the *Cambridge Historical Journal*, and I wish here to express my gratitude to the Editorial Board for kindly allowing them to be included in the present volume. I wish also to thank those who have assisted in the preparation of this work. My friends, Professor E. E. Stengel of the University of Marburg and Mr L. F. Salzman, M.A., F.S.A., have both by their kind interest and their practical suggestions contributed much towards its accomplishment, and I have received valuable help from Professor A. Hamilton Thompson of the University of Leeds. I also owe much to the help of my father, especially in correcting the proofs and making the index. To Dr G. G. Coulton, the editor of this series, who was my supervisor during the writing of the thesis on which this book is based, my debt of gratitude is naturally the greatest.

K. L. W.-L.

January 1934

CONTENTS

CHAPTER I

ROYAL ADMINISTRATION OF RELIGIOUS HOUSES

ONE of the most interesting exercises of the royal authority which the Patent Rolls disclose is the king's intervention in the affairs of certain financially embarrassed monasteries. The measures taken in a number of such cases have been described in detail in the accounts of individual religious houses published in the Victoria County Histories and elsewhere; but, so far, no attempt to study the question of royal intervention as a whole appears to have been undertaken. It is indeed a somewhat discouraging subject, for the evidence very frequently ceases just where it is most needed, and, consequently, the investigation seems to raise more problems than it solves. In spite of its defects, however, the evidence seemed sufficient to throw light on some points of interest concerning the internal affairs of the monasteries, and considerably to increase our knowledge of their relations to the king, and, consequently, an attempt to study the question of the royal intervention seemed to form a necessary part of the present work.

Here, as elsewhere, I shall deal mainly with the records of the reign of Edward III, though in this case my study has necessarily included a careful examination of the documents of the three preceding reigns. A similar investigation of the evidence subsequent to the reign of Edward III has not been possible. If it were undertaken it might considerably alter much that I have said here, especially as the end of Edward III's reign has been taken as a purely arbitrary limit to this enquiry and marks no important point in the development of the present problem. Therefore such conclusions as I have reached must be regarded as merely tentative.

When or how the custom by which the king came to interfere in the affairs of impoverished monasteries grew up I have not been able to discover. The earliest indications of such a custom which I have traced come from certain attempts on the part of

Henry III to relieve some monasteries of their debts or to check their extravagance. In November 1236, he issued a

> Request to the knights and freemen, as well burgesses as others, tenants of the abbey of Evesham, to discharge the abbey from debt out of regard for God and brother Richard, lately promoted to be abbot, for whom the king has a special regard; the state of the abbey having so changed that whereas it used to abound in goods, now it is not only destitute of them, but burdened with debt.[1]

From time to time also during the reign the tenants of other monasteries were requested by the king to grant them aids for the payment of their debts.[2]

In issuing letters of this kind the king was, of course, doing no more than giving the support of the royal approval to the levying of an extraordinary aid. Of much more importance for the present study is the unique measure by which, in 1255, he attempted to put an end to the excessive expenditure at Winchester. This took the form of a

> Notification to all merchants, citizens and others that the king wishes it to be known that the monks of the cathedral church of Winchester, putting no moderation to superfluous expenses, and exceeding the limits of bountifulness and the bounds of prodigality, have bound their church by so great debts to creditors that it is scarcely hoped in these days that they can be relieved from the burden thereof. The king therefore, although it should have been stopped at the beginning, so that the small spark should not leap to a destroying flame, prohibits anyone from making any loan, whether under the seal of the chapter or otherwise to the monks or to William de Tanton, who justly removed from the administration of the priory of that church still bears himself as prior.[3]

From measures such as this, the type of intervention which occurs most commonly in the later rolls may have developed. This was the issue of a royal commission, reciting that for certain specified causes the king had taken a particular monastery into his hands and committed its keeping to one or more persons who, after finding reasonable sustenance for the head of the house and the convent and their necessary servants and supporting other charges incumbent on the house, were to apply the remainder of the revenues towards the discharge of the monastery's debts or

[1] *Cal. Pat. Rolls*, 1232–47, p. 166.
[2] *Ibid.* 1266–72, p. 29.
[3] *Ibid.* 1247–58, p. 396.

towards its relief in other ways. The first instance of this type of intervention in the affairs of a monastery which has so far been noticed occurred in October 1255, when the king appointed

John de Ocketon, knight, Adam de Fraxino and Simon de Warrewik, monks of the abbey of St Mary, York, to keep that house which has fallen into debt; they having sworn before the king that they would keep it faithfully, and apply the issues and profits to the maintenance of the abbot and convent and their necessary household and the discharge of their debts of the abbey, and that they will desist from the showing of hospitality and other less necessary expenses until the house is out of debt.

The abbey was at the same time granted simple protection until it should be out of debt.[1]

As yet, however, the commissions had no regular form. In 1259, the abbey of Evesham was granted protection during pleasure, and "at the instance of the abbot and monks", Reynold de Inteberg, one of the monks, and Adam le Butiler were appointed "to keep the said abbey and the issues, for the discharge of its debts, and to render account yearly to the abbot and convent, with some one deputed on behalf of the king to audit the account".[2] The next record of the kind which the Patent Rolls contain is the appointment, in 1262,

of Stephen Fromund to see that no destruction of the goods or lands or dilapidation of the goods of the priory of St Swithun, Winchester, takes place, so nevertheless that the prior have free administration, without waste or destruction, of the manors and possessions assigned to his office for a moderate household and his steward, and that the convent has completely and honourably what it might and is accustomed to have, and that the residue fall to the discharge of the debts of the said house.[3]

A few other commissions to the same purpose, but differing widely in form from each other and from those already cited, were issued during the remaining years of Henry's reign; under his successors they appeared much more frequently, and their form gradually became more regular, until by the beginning of the reign of Edward III it varied as little as that of most other royal commissions.

[1] *Cal. Pat. Rolls*, 1247–58, p. 428.
[2] *Ibid.* 1258–66, p. 58. [3] *Ibid.* 1258–66, p. 196.

When, under Henry III, the first records of the appointment of custodians for financially embarrassed monasteries occur, they do not state to whom the patronage of these monasteries belonged. Most, if not all, of those which the king endeavoured to assist by such means were, in fact, of his patronage, but this circumstance was apparently regarded as too well known, or too little to the purpose, for mention in the commissions. The first reference to a royal foundation which the commissions contain is in 1293, when the abbot of Stanley was appointed to the custody of the temporalities of the priory of Amesbury, "founded by the king's ancestors".[1] Occasional references to royal foundation or patronage are to be found in the commissions issued under Edward II, but mention of the patronage does not become a regular part of the writ until the reign of Edward III, during whose time it was never omitted. Of the thirty-six monasteries on whose behalf Edward III issued one or more commissions, thirty-two were described as of royal foundation; two others, Waverley Abbey and the priory of Holy Trinity, York, were said to be *largely* of royal foundation, and the remaining two, West Dereham Abbey and Sherborne Priory, were of the patronage of the heirs of tenants-in-chief, whose lands and, consequently also, whose ecclesiastical patronage were at the time in the king's hands. These facts alone are sufficient to show that by the time of Edward III the possession of the patronage had become an important matter when the supervision of a monastery's finances was contemplated. Instructive also is the writ for an inquisition and the return made thereto concerning the alien priory of Lapley by Stafford. The three commissioners were enjoined to certify the king

by whom the priory was founded, and whether it is of the king's advowson; and, if so, with what rents and possessions it was endowed at its foundation, whether any of his progenitors ever had the custody of it during voidance, whether the priors have ever done fealty to his progenitors, and, if so, what hospitalities and alms the prior is bound by the foundation to give, and by what person or persons the present evils have been brought about.[2]

In this commission it is significant that the first question is whether the advowson belonged to the king, and that all the

[1] *Cal. Pat. Rolls*, 1292–1301, p. 18. [2] *Ibid.* 1334–38, p. 211.

other items appear to depend on the answer given to this question. What is still more important is, that after the commissioners' return, which described a most unsatisfactory state of affairs, but made it clear that the priory was not of the king's patronage,[1] no further action was taken in the matter, though, in the case of a royal foundation, a commission of enquiry which revealed defects was usually followed by the appointment of custodians and a grant of special protection.

Further evidence on this point comes from the endorsement of a petition which the English monks of the order of Cluny presented in the parliament of Winchester in 1330. The petition was mainly concerned with the alleged oppressions by the French priors and monks, and in it the English monks complained that their houses were badly ruled in spiritual and temporal affairs, to the great disgrace of the king, who was asked to provide a remedy for the evils described. On the back of this petition was written,

> Soyt maundé a les Abbes, & Priours del dit ordre, que sont del patronage del Roy en Engleterre qil facent hastife amendement des choses contenues en cest petition, in peril appertement issi, que le Roy ne admestre de metere la maine en autre manere. Et quant as Abbeis & Priories que sont de autre aduoere, nihil fiat.[2]

But the most important proof that the king's rights of intervention were limited to royal foundations is to be found in an item in the Chancery Warrants, in which it is stated that the king lately upon the suggestion of the prior of Thetford appointed a keeper of that house by letters patent by which the king's brother, Thomas, earl of Norfolk, is disturbed from doing what pertains to him, and the repeal of the letters patent was commanded, "if the patronage belongs to the earl".[3] These indications taken together form fairly conclusive proof that the king could, or would, intervene only in the affairs of those monasteries which were of royal patronage. Whether the king in issuing such commissions was conferring a favour, or exercising a right, is not clear. From the commissions already cited, and from others of

[1] *Cal. of Inquisitions, Miscellaneous*, II, 1458.

[2] C. Reynerus, *Apostolatus Benedictinorum in Anglia*, Appendix, part iii, No. LXVIII, p. 148.

[3] *Cal. of Chancery Warrants*, I, p. 407.

the same period, it would seem that the king's interference was, at that time, regarded as a somewhat novel proceeding. This is suggested by the variations in the wording of the commissions. Moreover, both Henry III and Edward I, in his early years, seem a little uncertain as to the extent to which the monks should be subjected to the royal commissioners. Thus, in the appointment of Stephen Fromund to see that no waste was committed at Winchester, it was stated that this was not to interfere with the prior's rights of administration of the estates which had been assigned to him, and again in 1275, when Edward I committed to Roland de Harlegh the custody of Leominster, an impoverished cell of Reading Abbey, he granted at the same time to the abbot and convent of Reading, "lest prejudice should arise to them hereafter, power to remove the said Roland from the custody at will".[1]

Such indications suggest that the king possessed no well-defined right to intervene in the affairs of an impoverished monastery. When he did so, it was probably regarded as largely, if not wholly, an act of special favour, and throughout the period under discussion the king's intervention retained something of this character, although he gradually acquired certain rights of interference. This is shown by the numerous instances in which the commission is said to have been issued at the request of the abbot and convent.[2]

In several other cases, the king's action seems to have been taken at the request of the abbot only,[3] or of the convent only,[4] and contrary to the will of the other party. Thus in May 1286 was issued a

> Notification of the king's will that Ralph de Brocton, king's clerk, lately appointed keeper of the abbey of Rading, the manor of Leominster and other manors of the said abbey, shall, notwithstanding contradiction of the convent or any other, apply with the counsel and consent of the abbot the revenues of the said abbey to the payment of its debts.[5]

In other cases the request for royal assistance clearly came from the convent and was made against the will of the abbot;

[1] *Cal. Pat. Rolls*, 1272–81, p. 128.
[2] *Ibid.* 1327–30, pp. 202, 302.
[3] *Ibid.* 1327–30, p. 302.
[4] *Ibid.* 1334–38, p. 175.
[5] *Ibid.* 1281–92, p. 242.

and again in the prolonged contest between the abbot of Wellow and his canons, the commissions suggest that each side had complained of the other to the king.[1] Whether the king, as patron, could have interfered when both the abbot and the convent opposed him, there is no means of knowing. Commissions to enquire concerning the defects of certain religious houses were occasionally issued, but these may have originated in complaints from some persons within the convents.

By the time of Edward II and Edward III attempts to safeguard the liberties of the monasteries or of their heads had been abandoned, and though, as in the earlier commissions, the abbot or prior and other members of the convent were often to advise the commissioners concerning the measures to be taken, it is fairly clear that until the commission was revoked the power of the custodians over temporal affairs was supreme. This change was probably due to certain legislation passed during the reign of Edward I, by which the king's position with regard to distressed monasteries was considerably altered, or, at any rate, much more clearly defined.

That which produced the most immediate effect was a clause contained in the first Statute of Westminster, by which it was decreed that none save the patron should be entertained in a religious house except at the invitation of its head.[2] This was directed against the custom by which nobles, royal officers, and other powerful persons with their retinues used to demand hospitality from the monasteries, where they frequently remained for long periods. The entertainment of such guests often involved the monasteries in serious financial difficulties, but, owing to the power of those who demanded it, to refuse was difficult, if not dangerous. It will be remembered that the custodians of St Mary's Abbey, York, had sworn before the king that they would desist from the showing of hospitality, and now the statute aimed at freeing all the monasteries from this burden. It was far from successful in putting an end to the abuse, as complaints addressed to king and pope throughout the Middle Ages testify, but this does not prove that the measure was altogether ineffective; for though it was constantly violated,

[1] *Cal. Pat. Rolls*, 1367–70, p. 7; 1370–74, p. 240.
[2] *Statutes of the Realm*, I, p. 26.

there can be no doubt that it was a means of protection in many individual cases of oppression. A convent which felt that demands for hospitality were proving too great a tax on its resources could now, in refusing such demands, invoke the real and moral support of the royal authority, and might petition the king for assistance against its unwelcome guests. Moreover, perhaps as a result of such petitions, the statute seems to have had an immediate effect on the measures taken for the relief of a number of impoverished monasteries. In 1275, the year in which this statute was published, the abbot of Reading received a mandate to remove from his abbey and from the cell of Leominster "all serjeants and horses with their keepers, either of the king or of others, staying in the said abbey or priory, and to receive no more until the said abbey shall have been relieved of its indebtedness".[1] The Patent Roll for the following year contains a prohibition to all persons from molesting or oppressing the abbey of Buildwas, contrary to the Statute of Westminster,[2] and in 1277, when Ralph de Sandwico, the king's steward, was appointed to the custody of Flaxley Abbey on account of that monastery's immense debts, the commission contained the clause that "no sheriff or other minister is to be lodged or intermeddle therein without special licence".[3] A clause to this effect appeared frequently during the remainder of the period under discussion, but not with sufficient regularity to seem part of the common form of the commissions, and this circumstance suggests that it was inserted only when the monastery in question was in need of its protection.

The second Statute of Westminster seems to have had an even more important, and a very direct, influence on the king's position with regard to impoverished monasteries. A clause in this statute decreed that if lands or rents which had been granted to religious houses for the maintenance of lights, chantries, or other works of piety, were alienated or otherwise misapplied, the grantor or his heirs might recover the gift.[4] A petition presented in the parliament of 1376,[5] and a number of inquisitions, which were ordered when neglect of works of piety for

[1] *Cal. Pat. Rolls*, 1272–81, p. 81.
[2] *Ibid.* 1272–81, p. 162.
[3] *Ibid.* p. 200.
[4] *Statutes of the Realm*, I, p. 92.
[5] *Rot. Parl.* II, p. 333.

which land had been granted was suspected,[1] prove that attempts were made to enforce this part of the statute. It was exactly calculated to justify the king's interference in the affairs of impoverished monasteries, since it empowered the benefactor of a monastery to take measures likely to ensure the performance of the established works of piety. Therefore, the statute, and the ideas which it engendered, seem gradually to have brought about an important change in the character, or at least in the avowed motives, of the king's intervention. It is perhaps significant that the first commission which mentions royal patronage was issued after the publication of the statute, and throughout the reign of Edward III the emphasis laid on the fact that the monasteries were of royal foundation was so constantly accompanied by the statement that chantries and alms which had been established for the souls of the king's progenitors and for the king had ceased or were in danger of being discontinued, as to suggest that the king's principal motive in endeavouring to assist the monasteries was to secure the resumption of the neglected works of piety. The prominence given to this aspect of the problem was, no doubt, largely due to the increasing interest in chantries and other works of piety done in the interest of individual souls, but if a legal basis for the king's action is to be found, it must be in a broad interpretation of the second Statute of Westminster.

So far, we have been considering the rights by which the king's intervention in the affairs of a monastery might be justified, and before going on to examine in detail the measures taken by the custodians whom he appointed, it will be necessary to give some attention to the conditions which they were expected to reform. Some evidence on this subject is to be found in the Papal Letters, but our principal sources of information are the records of the English Chancery, and particularly the commissions themselves. When the commissions are studied for this purpose, the first

[1] A particularly interesting commission of this class is that which directed "John de Brumwich, John Tracy, sheriff of Gloucester, and John de Sloghtre, to enquire by the oath of good men of the county of Gloucester of all chantries, alms, divine services and other pious works in abbeys, priories, churches and other places in the county which have been concealed or withdrawn and of the value of them; as the king has been given to understand very many such are concealed and withdrawn". *Cal. Pat. Rolls*, 1364–67, p. 71.

question that requires to be answered is, to what extent does the language describe the actual conditions of the monastery and to what extent is it mere common form? There is indeed a good deal of similarity in the language of most of the commissions and, as has already been suggested, their form tended to become more regular. The most striking indication that the wording of the commissions might be mainly common form occurs in 1354, when commissions were issued for the Augustinian priory of St Frideswide, Oxford, and for the Cistercian abbey of Meaux in terms so similar that the clerk enrolling the two items thought it sufficient to give the commission for St Frideswide's in detail, and then to write "Commission in like terms to [a group of custodians who are named] of the keeping of the abbey of Meaux".[1] It is quite likely, however, that the conditions existing in these two monasteries were really very similar, and it seems that the element of common form may easily be exaggerated. Different as were the causes which had led to the depressed state of the various monasteries, their financial condition at the time of the king's intervention was, probably, very similar, and therefore the constantly recurring phrases "loaded with debt" and "so that divine service will cease and the monks be dispersed unless a speedy remedy be applied" are probably, if allowance is made for the usual medieval exaggeration, fairly accurate descriptions of the actual state of affairs.[2]

Of far more importance than such phrases are the references to the causes of the monasteries' impoverishment. The earliest commissions stated only that a certain monastery had fallen into debt without attempting to account for the fact, but in 1269, when the abbey of Bileigh was taken into the king's hands, this was said to have been done by reason of contentions and discords between the abbot and the convent.[3] In the commissions of the time of Edward I and Edward II the misfortunes to which a monastery's impoverishment was attributed were occasionally mentioned, and, under Edward III, few commissions were issued

[1] *Cal. Pat. Rolls*, 1354–58, p. 51.

[2] Bishops also made use of common form in issuing their injunctions after their visitations, but, as Professor Hamilton Thompson has shown, this common form really described existing conditions. *Visitation of Religious Houses in the diocese of Lincoln*, II, p. xlviii (5).

[3] *Cal. Pat. Rolls*, 1266–72, p. 390.

which did not contain some allusion to the causes of the existing distress. Such information is, as a rule, far less detailed than one would wish, but it is sufficient to give a fairly clear idea of the difficulties with which the custodians would have to contend.

The hostility of the townsmen to the monasteries at the beginning of Edward III's reign was apparently responsible for the commissions on behalf of the two great abbeys of Abingdon and Bury St Edmunds,[1] though, a few years earlier, Abingdon had been in the hands of custodians on account of its debts.[2] The depressed state of Trentham and Croyland[3] was attributed to the hostility of men of the neighbourhood. The impoverishment of the priory of Holy Trinity, London, was ascribed to the refusal of its tenants to pay their accustomed services;[4] Netley and Bindon Abbeys complained that their situation on the sea coast exposed them to the attacks of the king's alien enemies and that their goods were wasted by mariners stopping there on their way to parts beyond the sea.[5] The depression of the Cistercian nunnery of Tarrant is attributed, in part, to an accidental fire,[6] and once, in the case of St Mary's Abbey, Winchester, the pestilence finds a place among the reasons given for the monastery's distress.[7] As a rule, however, such misfortunes were not regarded as the sole, or even the principal, cause of a monastery's decline. This was generally ascribed, wholly or in part, to misrule. The word occurs so frequently in the commissions for Edward III's reign that one would be inclined to treat it as mere common form were it not that some details in the commissions themselves, as well as much evidence from other documents, furnish abundant proof of the genuineness and the seriousness of this cause.

References to misrule did not indeed appear in any of the commissions belonging to the period before the reign of Edward III; though dissensions, which were probably the result of it, were mentioned in three of the nine cases in which the causes of the monastery's decline were specified. Under Edward III, misrule was said to be at least one of the reasons for the distress

[1] *Cal. Pat. Rolls*, 1327–30, pp. 127, 106.
[2] *Ibid.* 1317–21, p. 498.
[3] *Ibid.* 1343–45, pp. 253, 339.
[4] *Ibid.* 1358–61, p. 229.
[5] *Ibid.* 1345–48, p. 445; 1348–50, p. 52.
[6] *Ibid.* 1364–67, p. 239.
[7] *Ibid.* 1361–64, p. 485.

of twenty-three out of the thirty-six monasteries in whose affairs the king intervened. This should not be taken as indicative of a serious decline in monastic discipline or in the character of those appointed to govern the religious houses. It may suggest an increasing readiness to admit that the evil of misrule existed in the monasteries, but probably it was mainly due to the growth of the custom of stating the causes of impoverishment. Had they been described with equal regularity in the commissions of the earlier period, it is likely that these too would have contained many references to misrule. The commissions, therefore, do not provide material for a comparison of the state of the monasteries in the two periods.

A number of commissions merely state that a monastery's misfortunes were the result of misrule without explaining whether it was the fault of former presidents or of the existing head of the house. In others, "the misrule of past presidents" is the alleged cause of poverty, and in some of these cases, such as that of Bindon in Dorset, our knowledge of the careers of previous abbots shows that the complaint was fully justified, but in other instances one suspects that the abbot or prior who ruled the house when the commission was issued, was really to blame in great part at least. Thus, in 1366, when a custodian was appointed for the Cistercian monastery of Bordesley the impoverishment was said to be "owing to the misrule and carelessness of past presidents", and the king's intervention to have been undertaken "out of compassion for the state of the abbey and of John de Stoke, the abbot".[1] This suggests that John was not held responsible for any intentional waste of the monastery's goods, but the fact that he was not given even an advisory part in the management of the abbey's affairs under the custodian may indicate that he was thought incompetent, and the emphasis on the misrule of past presidents may be only a device to spare him the humiliation of confessing his inability to govern his house. This would be particularly likely if, as was often the case, the commission was based on a petition from the abbot and convent, and if the abbot was lacking in capacity for business rather than guilty of deliberate extravagance or misuse of the monastery's revenues. Incompetence probably often caused the

[1] *Cal. Pat. Rolls*, 1364–67, p. 245.

misrule complained of, and in some cases like that of Winchcombe in 1353,[1] when misrule is said to have been the reason for the king's intervention, and when the appointment of the custodians was made at the request of the abbot and convent, it is not unlikely that the head, realizing his incapacity, readily concurred in an arrangement which should greatly lessen his responsibilities.

In many cases, however, the extravagance or still more serious faults of the abbot or prior were said to have brought about the monastery's misfortunes. The hostility between the English and French monks in the alien priories may account for the statement, in a commission of 1331, that the priory of Holy Trinity, York, was "now grievously burdened with debt through the bad rule of the present prior, an alien, and of other priors",[2] but there are no similar circumstances which can be urged in defence of the other heads of religious houses whom the commissions accuse of misrule.

In 1368, the prior of St Frideswide's, Oxford, was alleged to have bound his priory "in such intolerable sums in parts beyond seas that the possessions and faculties of the priory, if those sums were to be paid, would not suffice to support the canons and the necessary charges of the priory".[3] The financial condition of this monastery had been, for many years, unsatisfactory. Recognizances of debts enrolled on the Close Rolls show that it had borrowed considerable sums both from English and from Italian merchants.[4] In September 1340, the prior had been granted a respite in the payment of certain tenths which had been granted by the clergy "because the goods of the priory do not suffice to pay the tenths and other quotas saving maintenance of the prior and convent";[5] and in May 1354, on account of the priory's debts, which were attributed to "misrule and other adversities", the king had granted it protection and entrusted the management of its affairs to two custodians.[6] In these circumstances, it is clear that the monastery was in no condition to bear extraordinary charges, yet heavy expenses which might have been altogether avoided were imposed as a result of the stupidity or

[1] *Cal. Pat. Rolls*, 1350–54, p. 481. [2] *Ibid.* 1330–34, p. 161.
[3] *Ibid.* 1367–70, p. 120.
[4] *Cal. Close Rolls*, 1337–39, p. 128; 1341–43, pp. 115, 679.
[5] *Ibid.* 1339–41, p. 625. [6] *Cal. Pat. Rolls*, 1354–58, p. 51.

baseness of one of its priors. The amount of the debts which had been contracted in parts beyond the seas is nowhere stated, but a probable explanation of the way in which they had been incurred is unexpectedly afforded by a letter which, in 1365, the Prince of Wales addressed to the pope. In this letter, the prince stated that

his chaplain, Nicholas de Hungerford, formerly prior of St Frideswide's, Oxford, obtained the priory and governed it for sixteen years, and then exchanged it with John de Dodeford, canon of Carlisle, for a certain vicarage, in which transaction the trickery of John and his own simplicity caused him unconsciously to be guilty of simony, and afterwards laid the matter before the pope, who issued a commission to the cardinal of Nîmes, who ordered the said Nicholas to be deprived both of the priory and vicarage: the pope is prayed to absolve Nicholas from the crime, which arose from his simplicity, and to rehabilitate and replace him in the said priory, or at least to recommit the matter to the cardinal of Nîmes, who is now better informed of the simplicity of Nicholas and the trickery of John.[1]

Litigation was a frequent cause of monastic poverty, and the expenses of a suit at the Roman Court such as the prince's letter describes, especially if it included providing that the cardinal should be "better informed concerning the simplicity of Nicholas", would be a serious burden on the resources of any house in the position of St Frideswide's.

In 1353, the indebtedness of Abbotsbury, a Benedictine house, was ascribed to "default of rule by the abbot",[2] and this statement, as we shall see later, was fully corroborated by other evidence.

Ten years earlier, the abbey of Middleton, which was also of the Benedictine order, was taken into the king's hands. According to the commission, it was in a state of great depression and indebtedness by reason of dissensions between the abbot and some of the monks.[3] In the commission, Richard Maury, who was then abbot, was not accused of misrule, but he was subsequently deposed, and in 1359 a commission consisting of four eminent lawyers was appointed to make an inquisition touching an information that brother Richard Maury "in the time when he was abbot and afterwards, destroyed, alienated, and wasted

[1] *Cal. Papal Petitions*, I, p. 509.
[2] *Cal. Pat. Rolls*, 1350–54, p. 536. [3] *Ibid.* 1343–45, p. 264.

the lands, rents and goods of the abbey and levied to his own use debts, farms and rents belonging to the same".[1] This is all that we can learn of the nature of Richard Maury's crimes, but he must have been guilty, or at least suspected, of some offence even greater than the spoliation of his abbey, for within a few days of the issue of the commission, the following remarkable letter was sent out from the English Chancery:

To the abbot of Cherteseye. Order, upon his allegiance, as he wishes to avoid the king's displeasure and upon pain of forfeiture, to keep brother Richard Maury, monk of the abbey of Middelton, so safely that he may not depart from that custody without the king's special order, so that the abbot may be able to answer for his body, as the king lately caused Richard, arrested for grave excesses, to the prejudice of the king and the said abbey, to be delivered, of his favour towards the Church and for the honour of religion, to that abbot and to the abbots of St Albans and Westminster, to be kept in close custody until further order, and now the king has learned that Richard is wandering at large without guard and proposes to go to parts beyond the sea, which might be to the prejudice both of the king and of the church.[2]

It would be easy to quote other instances of misrule,[3] but one further example must here suffice. In 1371, the king wrote to the bishop of Worcester commanding him "to repair in person to the abbey of St Augustine, Bristol, and to visit the same in the head and in the members". It had been found by divers inquisitions that the abbey

for lack of good governance and by neglect of Henry now abbot, who has brought it low as well by sale and conferment of corrodies, by hurtful demises to farm of the possessions thereof bringing little or no profit, by waste, sale and destruction of the said possessions, as by his excessive and fruitless expenses upon the manors, lands, rents, property and means thereof, is so burdened with debt that the worship of God is ceasing therein, alms and works of piety of old time appointed for the souls of the king's forefathers are withdrawn, and it is to be feared that the canons there dwelling are like to be dispersed through lack of sustenance.[4]

[1] *Cal. Pat. Rolls*, 1358–61, p. 217.
[2] *Cal. Close Rolls*, 1354–60, p. 551.
[3] See, *e.g.*, the references to Bruern, *Cal. Pat. Rolls*, 1364–67, pp. 86, 244, and to Stoneleigh, *ibid.* pp. 29, 133, 134, and *V.C.H. Warwick*, II, pp. 80, 81.
[4] *Cal. Close Rolls*, 1369–74, p. 259.

But however unfit to govern a monastery the head might be, the difficulties of removing him were great. In the case of Benedictine houses and those of other orders which were subject to episcopal control, the head could not be removed without the authority of the bishop of the diocese, while monasteries belonging to the exempt orders would usually have to obtain the assent of the abbot of a mother-house. Even when an abbot or prior had been successfully deposed, it was always possible for him to appeal for restitution to a higher authority, which was sometimes the court of the archbishop, but more often that of the pope. The litigation which would then ensue was certain to be costly, and it was likely to end in the restoration of the deposed president. When this happened, his vengeance was to be feared, particularly by those who had taken an active part in opposing him. Such fears are expressed in a petition which Robert de Stowe, a monk of Bruern Abbey, presented to the pope in 1363. In this he stated that he, on the part of his monastery, obtained the office of proctor in a cause of spoliation against John de Donsterre, formerly the abbot, "who has been restored to the possession of his monastery by the cardinal of Boulogne, auditor of the cause. Robert, fearing John's hatred and that of his complices, prayed leave to transfer himself to the monastery of Beaulieu".[1] One is glad to read that this petition was granted; for it is easy to imagine the misery which a vindictive abbot, returning victorious from Rome, might inflict on those who had sought to deprive him of his office and who were bound by their rule to spend all their days in the monastery which he governed.

But appeal to a higher court was not the only means which a deposed abbot might employ to procure his restoration or to take vengeance on the house of whose headship he had been deprived. In 1331, a commission issued on behalf of the Augustinian monastery of Lilleshall in Shropshire, stated that it had been impoverished "by reason of a quarrel between the present abbot and John de Chetwynde, the late abbot, who, after secretly withdrawing" from the monastery, "procured a band of persons to attack the abbey and remove the goods of the same to dissipate at their will".[2]

[1] *Cal. Papal Petitions*, I, pp. 470–1. [2] *Cal. Pat. Rolls*, 1330–34, p. 163.

Probably the most serious case of this kind which occurred during our period was at the small Cistercian monastery of Bindon in Dorset. The lack of ecclesiastical records relating to Cistercian houses renders it extremely difficult to determine the exact date or order of the events which took place there, but a number of entries on the Close and Patent Rolls make the principal points of the story fairly clear.

Sometime between 1316 and 1329, John de Monte Acuto became abbot of Bindon,[1] but at a Cistercian General Chapter he was deposed, probably for misrule, and one Roger put in his place. This sentence John apparently determined to resist by armed force. He and some of the monks who supported him seem to have withdrawn from the abbey and collected a band of armed followers, with whose help they attacked it. For a time their methods may have been successful, as a letter from the king to the abbot of Cîteaux, in which the events at Bindon are summarized, states that John had "entered into possession of the abbey by armed force and taken possession of, and dissipated the goods that he found there, distributing them among his aiders and abettors".[2] At any rate, by May 1329 the monastery had been taken into the king's hands "in consequence of a grievous dissension which has arisen on the question of the removal or change of the abbot, resulting in the carrying away of the goods of the abbey by a large mob, the withdrawal from the abbey of many of the monks and the cessation of divine offices and alms".[3] Several appointments of custodians for Bindon occur in the following years, and two commissions of Oyer and Terminer[4] testify to the convent's losses at the hands of lawless men of the neighbourhood. For a time John de Monte Acuto seems to have wandered about the country, but by May 1331[5] he and a fellow monk had been captured, apparently in or near London, and a writ of aid was issued on behalf of William Trussel and Richard de Kingston, a monk of Bindon, who were taking them back to the abbey, but he escaped from this custody, as we learn from a writ for his recapture which was sent out in August of the same year.[6] The letter to the abbot of Cîteaux, already cited, which was

[1] *V.C.H. Dorset*, II, p. 86.
[2] *Cal. Close Rolls*, 1330–33, p. 619.
[3] *Cal. Pat. Rolls*, 1327–30, p. 391.
[4] *Ibid.* 1330–34, pp. 131, 449.
[5] *Ibid.* 1330–34, p. 142.
[6] *Ibid.* 1330–34, p. 201.

written in 1332, says that John was then imprisoned in the abbey, but apparently he was still formidable, for the purpose of the letter was to inform the abbot of Cîteaux concerning John's misdeeds and to request that he with the other monks his accomplices, imprisoned in the abbey by reason of their faults, should be transmitted to places far distant to do perpetual penance. Moreover, since the abbot of Ford, to whom the house was subject by affiliation, encouraged John, the king asked the abbot of Cîteaux to reserve the affiliation and visitation to himself and to commit the visitation to a discreet abbot in whose industry he had confidence. I have not been able to discover what action the abbot of Cîteaux took in this matter, but nothing further is heard concerning John de Monte Acuto. His monastery remained burdened with debt and in frequent need of the king's special protection for a period of nearly thirty years, the last appointment of custodians occurring in 1357.[1] Its recovery was doubtless retarded by the frequent attacks of the king's alien enemies and by mariners calling there on their way to parts beyond the seas, of which the abbot and convent complained; and probably, too, the monastery suffered from the pestilence, though this is not mentioned in the commissions, but there can be little doubt that the misfortunes of Bindon in the fourteenth century were mainly due to the harm inflicted by its lawless abbot John.

Here it may be well to discuss briefly the evidence of these commissions as to the effect on the monasteries of the Black Death. Among the many causes to which the distress of the monasteries was attributed in these records, the pestilence, as has already been pointed out, was mentioned only once (in a commission of 1364, relating to the nunnery of St Mary's, Winchester),[2] and then misrule appears to have been equally responsible for the abbey's impoverishment. This fact is interesting in view of the emphasis laid on the pestilence in the ecclesiastical records of the period, and especially when one remembers that in most instances the causes of impoverishment, recited in the commission, were those to which the abbot and convent themselves, in their petition to the king, had assigned their misfortunes. It suggests that, though losses, suffered as a result of the

[1] *Cal. Pat. Rolls*, 1354–58, p. 565. [2] *Ibid.* 1361–64, p. 485.

plague, might be a sufficiently plausible reason for the need of appropriating a church, or securing some other concession which the ecclesiastical authorities could grant, it was necessary to plead some less general disaster in order to obtain the king's assistance. Nevertheless, if the consequences of the Black Death in reducing the revenues of the monasteries or in lowering the character of the monks had been as serious as some writers would lead us to suppose, we might reasonably expect to find an increase in the number of cases in which royal intervention was necessary. Such an expectation, however, is not fulfilled. During the entire reign of Edward III, sixty-six commissions on behalf of impoverished monasteries were enrolled; thirty-two in the years which preceded the pestilence, and thirty-four during the longer period which followed it. The commissions concerned thirty-six monasteries, of which eighteen were taken into the king's hands before the plague, but not afterwards; fourteen received this form of assistance for the first time—during our period—after the Black Death; and four (the Cistercian abbeys of Bindon, Bruern and Stanley and the Augustinian abbey of Lilleshall) were committed to custodians both before and after the plague. These figures, of course, are not intended to prove that the religious houses did not suffer from the pestilence. Royal intervention was probably an extreme measure which was adopted only when the condition of a monastery was particularly grave, and therefore the general prosperity of the monasteries might be considerably diminished without causing any increase in the number of houses which were assisted by the king. That the religious, like their secular neighbours, suffered heavy losses through the pestilence is undeniable, but the figures given above show that it did not increase the number of monasteries requiring royal assistance, and it appears, moreover, that the plague was not regarded as directly responsible for any of the most serious misfortunes which befell individual monasteries during our period.

From what has been said concerning the causes which led to the king's intervention in the affairs of the monasteries, it is clear that the task of the custodians must often have been difficult and can seldom have been pleasant. Yet there is no evidence that attempts were made to avoid fulfilling this duty of serving as a custodian, and it was probably accepted and performed as a matter of course in the same way as other local business was done.

Whether the custody of a monastery was profitable to the keepers there is no means of knowing. Only once is mention made of any payment to a keeper. This was in a commission to see that no waste was committed at the priory of St Swithin, Winchester, when Stephen Fromund, the custodian, was to receive from the goods of the priory, "his necessaries for himself and two or three mounts (*equitaturis*) at most, when he goes to the places belonging to the priory".[1] This is, of course, no more than a modest allowance towards the expenses which his services to the priory would involve, but there is no proof that similar provision was made for other custodians, though probably the commissioners received hospitality from the monasteries which they were endeavouring to assist. It is possible, however, that while managing the temporal affairs of a religious house, the custodians may have perceived and availed themselves of opportunities for adding to their own incomes. But if they did so, no record of their proceedings is now extant. The only evidence of a complaint against custodians which I have discovered is contained in a commission of 1321 which appointed

> Geoffrey de Somersete, sub-prior of Bermondsey, and William de Alingeo, parson of the church of Newenton, to the custody of the priory of Bermondsey, the prior and convent thereof having complained that as regards Master Robert de Haselshawe, provost of Wells, and John de Lodelowe, monk of the said priory, lately appointed keepers, the former takes no part and the latter does not behave well in the custody thereof.[2]

In this case, however, no definite charge was brought against John de Lodelowe, and whatever may have been his offences they were not sufficiently serious to prevent his being again appointed in 1332 as one of the custodians of the priory.[3]

The men to whom the custody of monasteries was entrusted were drawn from several of the higher social classes. From the beginning, laymen seem to have served quite as often as ecclesiastics. It will be remembered that in the commission of 1255

[1] *Cal. Pat. Rolls*, 1258–66, p. 196.
[2] *Ibid.* 1321–24, p. 23.
[3] *Ibid.* 1330–34, p. 332.

which was issued on behalf of St Mary's Abbey, York, one of the custodians was John de Ocketon, knight, and I have been able to discover only one statement of objection to the practice. This occurs in 1270, when John de Cobham, to whom the king had committed the keeping of the priory of Higham, was removed, and John de Witham, king's chaplain, put in his place "as the king thinks it more seemly to commit it to an ecclesiastic",[1] but the force of even this mild objection is greatly diminished by the fact that a few weeks later Higham was again in lay custody.[2] Ecclesiastical keepers were, in fact, far less prominent than might have been expected, and their number tended to diminish. Of the ecclesiastics who were appointed, only a small proportion were Religious. In a few instances, one or more members of the house concerned were mentioned by name among the commissioners; and the heads of other religious houses occasionally served. The abbots of Ford and of Beaulieu were among the custodians of Bindon;[3] the abbots of Waverley, Rewley and Thame were, in 1365, appointed with three laymen to the custody of Bruern Abbey.[4] In 1332, the prior of Stanesgate and John de Lodelowe, a monk of Bermondsey, were the keepers of that priory;[5] and in 1335, when the Cistercian house of Flaxley was taken into the king's hands on account of its debts, its custodians were the abbots of Bordesley and Dore and its prior.[6] It is perhaps noteworthy that, when the heads of religious houses were appointed as custodians, they were always men of the same order as the monks whom they were to assist. From time to time, the bishop of the diocese was one of the keepers of a monastery, but the majority of ecclesiastical keepers who were not monks were king's clerks, to whom the task was probably assigned rather because they were royal officials than because they were members of the clergy.

Some of the lay custodians were magnates of great importance. Hugh de Courtenay, earl of Devon, and his son, Hugh, were prominent among the protectors of Bindon Abbey;[7] Richard, earl of Arundel, was one of the custodians of the Cistercian monastery of Buildwas,[8] and Guy de Brian served on three

[1] *Cal. Pat. Rolls*, 1266–72, p. 444.
[2] *Ibid.* 1266–72, p. 452.
[3] *Ibid.* 1330–34, pp. 19, 406.
[4] *Ibid.* 1364–67, p. 86.
[5] *Ibid.* 1330–34, p. 332.
[6] *Ibid.* 1334–38, p. 175.
[7] *Ibid.* 1330–34, p. 19.
[8] *Ibid.* 1345–48, p. 110.

commissions for monasteries in the vicinity of his lands.[1] In 1344, William de Bohun, earl of Northampton, was appointed with the archbishop of Canterbury to assist Croyland Abbey;[2] while, about the same time, Thomas Wake of Lydell, who, according to the monks of Croyland, was largely responsible for the misfortunes of their house, received a similar commission for the Cistercian monastery of Louth Park.[3] But the most distinguished custodian of a monastery was John of Gaunt, who in 1365 was one of the keepers of Stoneleigh Abbey, and in 1377 was the sole keeper of the priory of St Frideswide, Oxford.[4]

It seems clear that, as a rule, the keepers were supposed to give their personal attention to the affairs of the distressed monastery. This is shown in a letter of 1270 to Master Ralph de Fremlingham, which stated that "In view of the fact that he is continually attendant to the business of the king's son Edward, and cannot conveniently attend to the keeping of the priory of Hecham which the king lately committed to him during pleasure, the king has committed that to Gilbert, dean of Sorham".[5] And some circumstantial evidence from the reign of Edward III supports the view that usually the custodians themselves fulfilled the duties imposed by their commission.

But it can hardly have been expected that bishops or important lay magnates would personally perform the duties of custodians. In 1270, when the earliest instance of a magnate's appointment occurs, it was said that the king had committed the keeping of Higham Priory to his brother Richard, king of Almain, on condition that he should substitute someone in his place to keep it.[6] Moreover, in 1293, when the abbot of Stanley was appointed to keep the temporalities of the house of Amesbury he was granted power to appoint a substitute when he could not attend.[7] If the head of a neighbouring monastery could thus be permitted to act by deputy, a similar concession would seem even more likely to be allowed in the case of the chancellor and bishop of Winchester, John Stratford, or of John of Gaunt at the end of Edward III's reign. The commissions,

[1] *Cal. Pat. Rolls*, 1350–54, p. 481; 1354–58, p. 39; 1374–77, p. 111.
[2] *Ibid.* 1343–45, p. 339.
[3] *Ibid.* 1343–45, p. 336.
[4] *Ibid.* 1364–67, p. 134; 1374–77, p. 452.
[5] *Ibid.* 1266–72, p. 410.
[6] *Ibid.* 1266–72, p. 452.
[7] *Ibid.* 1292–1301, p. 18.

however, contain no further instances of a custodian's being empowered to appoint substitutes, though when a commission was addressed only to one or two men of exceptionally high rank, we may safely assume that most, if not all, of the work which it entailed was performed by the magnate's subordinates. There are, however, very few cases in which the keeping of a monastery was entrusted solely to magnates, and their association in the commissions was probably intended to give added authority, while the actual business would be carried on by the less distinguished keepers. A similar practice was followed in appointing the justices of the peace of our period; for it was customary to make the judges and nobles commissioners of the peace in every county in which they held lands, but it is certain that the duties of the office were fulfilled by the knights and esquires with whom they were associated.

Of the laymen of less exalted rank to whom the keeping of monasteries was committed, some were eminent lawyers. James de Woodstock, a judge of the King's Bench, was in 1340 one of the keepers of Sherborne Priory;[1] Walter Perle, who became a king's serjeant, was associated in the commission of 1375 for the nunnery of Tarrant;[2] Simon de Kegworth, at the time king's attorney, was one of the custodians of the priory of Holy Trinity, London;[3] while the chief justice, Sir William Shareshull, was appointed to assist in the relief of four monasteries, Bruern, Lilleshall, St Frideswide's, Oxford, and Holy Trinity, London.[4] A few other keepers, such as Richard de Stafford, seem to have been knights particularly attached to the royal service, but the largest number belonged to the local gentry, and were the type of men who served as sheriffs and justices of the peace, and who represented their shires in parliament.

In many cases it is not clear what reasons governed the choice of the custodians. Probably they were often men who were known to be friends of the monastery. Sometimes, at least, they were suggested in the petition which the abbot and convent sent to the king. Thus in 1328, Gilbert de Ellesfeld and Thomas de Coudray were appointed to keep the abbey of Abingdon at the

[1] *Cal. Pat. Rolls*, 1340–43, p. 12. [2] *Ibid.* 1374–77, p. 111.
[3] *Ibid.* 1358–61, p. 229.
[4] *Ibid.* 1350–54, p. 62; 1354–58, p. 39; 1361–64, p. 462; 1350–54, p. 177; 1354–58, p. 51; 1358–61, p. 229.

request of the abbot and convent;[1] in 1353, the custodians of Winchcombe were appointed "with the consent of Reynold, bishop of Worcester...and at the request of the abbot and convent";[2] and in 1351, when Lilleshall was taken into the king's hands, it was committed to William de Shareshull, the chief justice, and William Banister of Yorton, "in whom both he [the king] and the abbot and convent have confidence".[3] In other cases, though no reason for the choice is given in the commission, it may be explained by circumstances in the previous history of the house. In 1352, one of the custodians of Bindon was John de Novo Burgo,[4] who seems to have been a country gentleman of Dorset. No indication is given as to why John was chosen for this task, but Bindon acquired the name and position of a royal foundation through the use which the convent had made of the founder's licence to choose their patron. The real founder who granted this privilege was Henry de Novo Burgo.[5] The family's connection with the monastery probably continued, and during the period of its misfortunes, John de Novo Burgo may well have been chosen to assist it, because he had, or was thought to have, a special interest in its welfare. Again in 1330, when Waverley Abbey was in need of assistance, the keeping of it was entrusted to John, bishop of Winchester,[6] whose predecessors had long been among the abbey's chief benefactors.[7]

The choice of the custodians seems to some extent to have been influenced by a consideration of the particular evils which they were intended to remedy. The appointment, in 1347, of the military knight Walter Manny to the keeping of Netley when a principal cause of that abbey's impoverishment was the practice of "mariners calling there and passing over to foreign parts"[8] was perhaps made in the hope that a soldier of his importance might be its most effective protector. It is probable, too, that Simon de Kegworth and William de Shareshull were chosen to assist the priory of Holy Trinity, London, whose tenants refused their accustomed rents,[9] because of a special need of the help which lawyers could give. And it is noteworthy that in a number

[1] *Cal. Pat. Rolls*, 1327–30, p. 202.
[2] *Ibid.* 1350–54, p. 481.
[3] *Ibid.* 1350–54, p. 177.
[4] *Ibid.* 1350–54, pp. 249, 250.
[5] *Ibid.* 1272–81, p. 357.
[6] *Ibid.* 1330–34, p. 26.
[7] *V.C.H. Surrey*, II, pp. 85–6.
[8] *Cal. Pat. Rolls*, 1345–48, p. 445.
[9] *Ibid.* 1358–61, p. 229.

of cases in which corrodies and farms were to be withdrawn or the payment of debts deferred beyond the time originally agreed upon, an eminent lawyer or some royal official who would be equally conversant with the best means of effecting these measures was one of the custodians.

The efforts of the custodians and of the monks to improve a monastery's financial condition were aided by a grant of special protection for the abbot and convent and their possessions, which usually formed a part of the letters appointing the keepers, or was issued at the same time as their commission. Such protection seems, in itself, to have been of assistance to a distressed monastery, as on several occasions during the reign of Edward III it was granted to houses for which custodians were not appointed. Thus the Cistercian monastery of Newminster was twice taken under the king's special protection when it was in a depressed state on account of the forays of the Scots, "and by divers men daily lodging in it and in its manors and granges against the will of the abbot".[1] Similarly, in 1341, the priory of Tynemouth was granted protection for so long as the war with Scotland should last, as it had been impoverished by the wars and "by the coming thither of magnates and others and making stay there",[2] and, in 1351, Dunmow Priory secured special protection "in consideration of the great depression in which that house now is by damage inflicted by men of those parts scheming to destroy it".[3]

Moreover, from 1275 onward, as we have seen, the simple protection was often accompanied by the clause forbidding the entertainment of royal officers and others or the carrying away of the monastery's goods. In 1325 the protection granted to the Augustinian abbey of Wellow by Grimsby was issued with the clause *nolumus*.[4] This clause, which had long been issued on behalf of other persons, expressly forbade the taking of the goods belonging to those to whom it was granted for the use of the king or of any other. (Nolumus etiam quod de bladis fenis equis carectis carriagiis victualibus, aut aliis bonis et catellis ipsius [A] contra voluntatem suam ad opus nostrum aut aliorum per

[1] *Cal. Pat. Rolls*, 1327–30, p. 309; 1334–38, p. 7.
[2] *Ibid.* 1340–43, p. 129. [3] *Ibid.* 1350–54, p. 136.
[4] *Ibid.* 1324–27, p. 153.

baillivos seu ministros nostros aut alterius cuiuscumque quicquid capiatur.) On this first occasion when the clause formed a part of the letters patent on behalf of a distressed monastery, the clause prohibiting royal officials and others from obtaining hospitality from the canons also appears, but thereafter only one clause or the other was used. During the early years of Edward III's reign the older clause appeared on several occasions, though the clause *nolumus* is found much more frequently, and soon altogether took the place of the former, which last appeared in the commission of 1351 for Lilleshall Abbey.[1] The change probably came about because in the royal chancery it was found more convenient to write the clause *nolumus*, the form of which was apparently invariable, and which for purposes of enrolment at least could be summarized in a single word, than to use the special clause which could be issued only on behalf of monasteries and which seems never to have acquired a fixed form. The meaning of the two clauses was very similar, and it seems likely that the clause *nolumus* gave equally effective protection to the monasteries in exempting them from the exactions of royal officers and from the necessity of showing hospitality.

In the commission in 1329, for Bermondsey Priory, the protection was granted with the clause *volumus*, by which it was definitely protected from many suits and pleas, including those of debt. Such a respite must have been a great advantage to an indebted house, but the clause does not appear in the commissions which were issued on behalf of other monasteries. In some cases the king's intervention may have been intended to secure for a monastery some alteration in the terms on which its debts were to have been repaid. This seems to be the meaning of the commission which in 1375 was issued on behalf of the abbey of Tarrant, in which the king's reason for having taken it into his hands was said to be "on information that the late abbess...has bound the abbey in such great sums to creditors in divers counties that the possessions thereof, if the sums be paid at the fixed terms, will not suffice for the sustenance of the nuns".[2] The king might also order that debts which had been illegally contracted should not be paid. In 1367 a commission concerning Wellow by Grimsby attributed that monastery's mis-

[1] *Cal. Pat. Rolls*, 1350–54, p. 177. [2] *Ibid.* 1374–77, p. 111.

fortunes to the misconduct of certain of the canons, "who neglect to obey the abbot's rule, borrow divers sums of money from men of Grymesby without the abbot's assent, charge the abbey with the said sums, cause the abbot to be impleaded for the same before the bailiffs of Grymesby, and bring divers other evils on the house", and commanded "that the abbey be not charged with sums borrowed as above, nor any distraint made for the same".[1] A similar measure may have been contemplated on behalf of St Frideswide's when it was said that the king had taken the priory into his hands because the prior had bound his priory "in such intolerable sums in the parts beyond seas that the possessions and faculties of the priory, if those sums were to be paid, would not suffice to support the canons and the necessary charges of the priory".[2] Here it was not explicitly stated that the payment of the debts was to be prevented, though this seems to be implied in the phrase "if those sums were to be paid". There is no proof that the debts had been illegally contracted in an ordinary sense, but since the money was owed in parts beyond the seas, its payment might be stopped by the enforcement of the laws which forbade the sending of money out of the realm.

Towards the end of the period under discussion the support of royal authority was also employed for the temporary or permanent revocation of leases of lands or grants of corrodies which seemed to have been made contrary to the interests of the house. The first occasion on which such measures were enjoined was in April 1364, when the king committed the keeping of St Mary's Abbey, Winchester, to William, bishop of Winchester. Its poverty was ascribed to a number of causes, which included its being "heavily charged with corrodies and sustenances", and the commission ordered that "all corrodies etc. are to cease until the house be relieved and the king give other order touching them, and all men and women dwelling in the abbey whose stay there is not necessary expelled...and the bishop is not to be impleaded in respect of the cessation of corrodies and expulsions".[3] During the remaining years of Edward III's reign

[1] *Cal. Pat. Rolls*, 1367–70, p. 7.
[2] *Ibid.* 1367–70, p. 120.
[3] *Ibid.* 1361–64, p. 485.

similar commands were issued with regard to five other monasteries, the abbeys of Stoneleigh, Bruern, St Augustine's, Bristol, Bordesley and Tarrant,[1] but in all of these cases some such phrase as "corrodies granted to suspected persons of foul character" or "corrodies sold and conferred on persons suspected of ill fame" appears, and in each instance the custodians were commanded to expel all suspected persons staying there. It may well be that the persons who had obtained the corrodies were really unsuitable inmates for a monastery, but it seems probable also that references to their bad characters were inserted to facilitate the repudiation of the corrodies. For if the abbot and convent had sold or granted a corrody in due form, it is difficult to see how it could legally have been withdrawn merely because the bargain was proving disadvantageous to the monastery. The stipulation in the commission for St Mary's, Winchester, that the bishop was not to be impleaded in respect of the cessations of the corrodies and the expulsions, shows that a corrody which had been granted according to the proper legal form could not, as a rule, be arbitrarily withdrawn, and that if this was attempted the corrodian might be expected to sue those who had deprived him. If, however, it could be shown that the characters of the corrodians made them unfit to dwell within the precincts of a monastery, they might be expelled on moral grounds. The suspicion that charges of immorality were thus employed to assist in bringing about what were really financial reforms is aroused by the fact that in all the commissions which mention corrodies conferred on persons of bad character, there are also references to profitless leases of the monastery's possessions, which are to be revoked.

The leases which were to be revoked were merely described as having been made contrary to the interests of the house, and nothing is said as to the legality either of these or of the corrodies. It is, however, noteworthy, that in all the commissions which enjoin the withdrawal of corrodies or leases, the existing head of the house or his predecessors were accused of misrule, a circumstance which suggests that they may have been illegally granted. If, in such transactions, the abbot had failed to secure the assent of the convent, or if any other irregularity in the form

[1] *Cal. Pat. Rolls*, 1364–67, pp. 29, 225, 244, 245; 1374–77, p. 111.

could be discovered, the repudiation of the corrodies and leases would probably be easy. Whether the grant of a corrody or lease which had been made without the consent of the patron of the house concerned was valid, there is no means of deciding. A monastery of royal foundation seems to have been bound to obtain a royal licence before it could permanently alienate any of its property, and at some religious houses this rule appears to have been so strictly observed that royal confirmations were sought and obtained even for the manumission of a villein.[1] A similar rule may have been observed with regard to temporary diminutions of monastic property, which the grants of leases or corrodies would involve. This is indicated by the numerous confirmations of leases and licences to lease monastic possessions which the Patent Rolls contain. Grants of corrodies, too, frequently received royal confirmation, though no licences to grant them occur, and of those which were confirmed, a considerable number had been conferred by alien priories, whose finances were more strictly under the king's control than those of other monasteries. A corrody paid by an alien priory might diminish the farm which it could pay to the king, and that this consequence was feared is shown by some of the letters patent in which the corrodies were confirmed provided that the king's farm was not thereby diminished.[2] Similarly, in the case of other monasteries where the king possessed the right of keeping the temporalities in times of voidance, corrodies and leases may have diminished his profits at such times, and he may also have claimed a right to interfere, if such grants were preventing the performance of works of piety, for which he or his ancestors had endowed the monasteries. These matters, however, are mere speculations, and, at present, it is impossible to decide whether the king, in ordering the withdrawal of corrodies and leases, was protecting the monasteries from the consequences of illegal acts or employing the royal power to nullify agreements which his courts would otherwise have regarded as binding.

It is clear, however, that as a rule the object of the king's intervention was to enable a monastery to discharge its obligations, not to free it from the necessity of fulfilling them. The

[1] *Cal. Pat. Rolls*, 1340–43, p. 561; 1350–54, p. 186; 1374–77, pp. 35, 187.
[2] *Ibid.* 1338–40, p. 272; 1354–58, p. 465.

first charges on the revenues of a religious house were recognized to be the provision of reasonable maintenance for the head and the convent and the support of the established works of piety, especially the distribution of alms to the poor. Usually, also, allowance for the cost of necessary servants was coupled with the provision for the abbot and convent, though in one case, that of Middleton in 1344, the "necessary expenses of the ministers of the house" were apparently to be found after the other charges had been met and "if the revenues suffice for this".[1]

To maintain as nearly as possible the appointed number of monks, and to perform the established works of piety, were duties which the abbot and convent owed to their patron and other benefactors, and the neglect of which would imperil the latter's souls. Yet in times of distress, the temptation to economize by withholding alms, allowing chantries to be discontinued, or reducing the number of monks, must have been great, and there is much evidence to show that it was a temptation to which the convents often yielded. In interfering in the affairs of a monastery, therefore, the king's main purpose was, probably, in many cases at least, to see that the appointed divine services and alms were not diminished, but either because the cessation of works of piety was to be feared so long as a monastery remained burdened with debt, or because it was also to the king's advantage to protect the interests of the creditors, he insisted that the debts of the abbot and convent must be paid. The commissions almost invariably ordered that after the above-mentioned charges had been met the remainder of the monastery's revenues should be applied towards the discharge of its debts, or else, omitting all mention of the expenses of the house, merely commanded that the profits should be spent in the payment of the debts. Indeed, the phrases relating to the reasonable maintenance of the abbot and convent and their necessary servants, while they may have been introduced partly to protect the monks from too severe a regime which zealous custodians might have enforced, were evidently intended to make it clear that the monks were to receive only reasonable sustenance, and that none but necessary servants were to be employed. This is shown by a

[1] *Cal. Pat. Rolls*, 1343–45, p. 264.

mandate which in 1285 was sent to Peter de la Mare, the constable of Bristol Castle, informing him that

the debts of the abbot and convent of St Augustine's, Bristol, are so great that unless the expenses of the house are curtailed, they cannot be paid, and directing him, with the advice of the abbot, prior, chamberlain and other elders of the house, to remove all unnecessary members of the household, to retrench the expenditure, to collect the revenues by one or two canons deputed for this purpose, and to apply the same subject to reasonable maintenance of the house to the payment of the said debts.[1]

These instructions are exceptionally explicit, but it seems fairly certain that the custodians who received less definite orders were expected to introduce similar reforms.

Such directions imply that if the revenues of a monastery were properly administered there would be a surplus out of which its debts could be paid, and the correctness of this supposition is established by much evidence from episcopal registers and other sources. The subject of monastic debts has already been discussed at some length by Mr R. H. Snape, who cites a number of cases in which an able abbot, within a few years of his election, succeeded in paying off the entire debt, sometimes amounting to a great sum, with which his house was burdened, and concludes that more careful management would, in many instances, have saved the monasteries from the necessity of contracting loans.[2] The task of the custodians, then, though it must often have been difficult, was by no means hopeless, and they appear to have been left free to accomplish it in whatever way they thought best. The instructions contained in the original commissions were, as we have seen, given in very general terms, with few suggestions as to how the desired economies were to be effected, and further orders to the custodians, after a monastery had once been committed to them, appear but seldom. The commission of 1344, for the abbey of Middleton, did indeed mention five marks as the amount that ought to be allowed annually for each monk,[3] but in all other cases it seems that the keepers themselves must have decided what should constitute "reasonable maintenance" and how many servants would be regarded as a "moderate number".

[1] *Cal. Pat. Rolls*, 1281–92, p. 198.
[2] R. H. Snape, *English Monastic Finances*, pp. 133–5.
[3] *Cal. Pat. Rolls*, 1343–45, p. 264.

The absence of precise directions in the commissions renders it extremely difficult for the modern student to see exactly how the custodians were expected to set to work, and very little evidence concerning their administration is extant. Several monasteries which were taken into the king's hands have left to us chronicles describing the years during which the custodians must have served, and one might reasonably hope that they would contain some references to the keepers and to the measures adopted under their guidance. But these matters the chroniclers entirely ignored, and other monastic records are not more informing. There is, however, just sufficient evidence to prove that the custodians were not inactive. The complaint of Bermondsey Priory against Robert de Haselshawe, the provost of Wells, that "he takes no part in the custody" is in itself a strong indication that the keeper's task was no sinecure, and this view is supported by the few glimpses of the work of the custodians which our documents afford.

The procedure which the custodians on being appointed would adopt is one of the many aspects of the present subject concerning which we have no evidence. The keepers, or some of their number, must have visited the house entrusted to them and, often with the help of some members of the convent, have drawn up a scheme of retrenchment. Probably the arrangements made varied considerably according to the circumstances which had led to the monastery's impoverishment, but we do not know all that was done or attempted even in a single instance. When the commissions had contained definite instructions, such as that grants of corrodies and leases were to be revoked, it may be assumed that some attempt was made to execute these orders. The Patent Rolls show that a corrodian of St Mary's, Winchester, and one of the lessees of land belonging to Stoneleigh Abbey, secured royal confirmation of their grants[1] about the time when the revocation of corrodies and leases had been commanded. This fact seems to indicate that their withdrawal was really to be feared, but it also shows that, in this, as in many other medieval regulations, the individual might, by purchase or favour, obtain exemption from compliance with the general order, and as we cannot discover how many corrodians and lease-holders were

[1] *Cal. Pat. Rolls*, 1361–64, p. 484; 1364–67, p. 178.

ejected, or for what considerations others were allowed to remain in possession, it is impossible to say to what extent the king's commands in such matters actually benefited the monasteries.

The constantly repeated order for "a moderate number of servants" cannot have been without effect. Episcopal registers and other records show that the keeping of too many servants was one of the commonest forms of monastic extravagance, and the removal of those who were not necessary was frequently enjoined after the bishop's visitation.[1] If then, as must often have happened, the custodians found a monastery burdened by an excessive number of servants, the dismissal of as many as could be spared would be one of the most effective measures of economy that could be introduced. But it would also be a difficult measure, and one most likely to cause friction between the monks and those sent to aid them; for the interpretation of "a moderate number of servants" which an extravagant abbot and convent would give would naturally be very different from the meaning attached to the phrase by the custodians, whose object was to reduce expenses and who would lose nothing of comfort or dignity by the economy. Nevertheless, when a party within the monastery favoured a policy of retrenchment, the keepers' decisions were probably enforced.

Expenses might be further reduced if the head of the house could be persuaded or compelled to give up for a time his separate household, or if he would withdraw from the monastery and live in retirement on one of its manors or elsewhere. The abbot's withdrawal may seem at first a doubtful economy, but in his absence the demands for hospitality from the monastery were probably fewer, and those guests who were received might be entertained in a less costly manner. Moreover, the head of a religious house would doubtless find it much easier to reduce the number of his attendants and generally to adopt a simpler style of living when he was not personally presiding over his monastery. At any rate, on several occasions the head of a religious house sought and obtained the king's permission to live away from his monastery as a means of improving its financial condition. An interesting example of this is afforded by letters

[1] For a discussion of this see Snape, *English Monastic Finances*, pp. 13–18.

patent which, in 1364, were issued on behalf of the abbot of Reading. In these he was granted

> Licence for one year...to leave his abbey and go to his cell at Leomynstre, co. Hereford, to stay there with a few household servants; on his petition showing that he cannot conveniently carry out works necessary for the repair of the church of Redynges and his abbey as well as in his manors and granges in those parts unless he act prudently and moderate his expenses.[1]

Reading and the other monasteries whose heads obtained such grants were not, at the time, in the king's hands and their decisions were probably made voluntarily, or at the suggestion of the convents, but without pressure from outside. Whether the presidents of religious houses which were in the king's hands often left their monasteries for this purpose during the period of custody, there is not sufficient evidence to decide, but since, at the time, the practice was recognized as a useful financial expedient, we may be fairly certain that from time to time it was employed, though the record of only one instance has come down to us. This record is a letter close concerning St Frideswide's, Oxford, which, in 1374, was directed to the keepers of that priory. In it they were ordered

> to deliver to brother John de Walyngford, prior thereof for his abode a place near Oxford called "Bunseye chapele" and of the issues of the priory...to pay him 6*s*. a week for his commons and the commons of a canon his fellow dwelling with him, 23*s*. 4*d*. a quarter for his raiment and the said canon's, 12*d*. a week for their servants' meat, and 5*s*. a quarter for their servants' wages, delivering to him hay, litter, and provender for one horse for his riding; as of his compassion for the said prior's estate the king has granted him to have that place for his dwelling and the dwelling of a canon with him and of their servants, and to take for his commons 4*s*. a week and for his raiment one mark a quarter, for the said canon's commons 2*s*. a week and for his raiment 10*s*. a quarter as other canons have in that house, and other the weekly and quarterly sums aforesaid.[2]

This document does not indeed explain how the sums to be spent on the prior and his fellow canon had been determined, but the amounts assigned to the latter were said to be the same as those which the other canons of the house received, and from the fact that the priory had, for some time, been under the super-

[1] *Cal. Pat. Rolls*, 1361–64, p. 504. [2] *Cal. Close Rolls*, 1374–77, p. 48.

vision of keepers, we may fairly assume that the canons' portions had been fixed by them, or at any rate with their assent. It is interesting to observe that even under this regime, which was apparently intended to be economical, the food allowance for the prior was twice that of his fellow canon, and that the cost of the canon's food was estimated at twice the amount that was thought sufficient for their servants. The prior, even when living in retirement at Binsey, where he can have been under no necessity of dispensing hospitality, was to be allowed to spend over ten pounds a year on his table; more in fact than the apparently liberal estimate for the entire maintenance of a monk at the university, while the estimated cost of the food and dress of each canon was nearly twice the legal stipend of a secular chaplain of the period.[1] These allowances for the members of a convent in the distressed condition of St Frideswide's seem excessive, especially when it is remembered that the canons were, in theory, bound to a life of poverty, but they may have represented a considerable reduction as compared with previous expenditure. Moreover, the financial interests of a house may have been better served when the custodians introduced a moderate plan of reform, to which the Religious would agree, than when they attempted to enforce a stricter economy which would arouse opposition. More drastic measures were adopted at Abbotsbury, the only other monastery concerning whose administration by custodians we have information, and our exceptional knowledge of its affairs is entirely due to the difficulties which the custodians encountered.

This monastery, because its goods were wasted through "default of rule by the abbot", was in December 1353 taken into the king's hands and its keeping committed to "Robert de Faryndon and Henry de Tolre, monks of the house, Walter Waleys, clerk, Thomas Cary and John de Munden",[2] who seem to have been prominent laymen of the neighbourhood. They instituted a plan of retrenchment, of which an important part was to order that the abbot should give up his separate chamber, and that all the convent should live together in one convenient building until the abbey should have been relieved. These details we learn from a petition which the custodians addressed

[1] *Rot. Parl.* II, p. 271. [2] *Cal. Pat. Rolls*, 1350–54, p. 536.

to the king's chancellor, complaining that the abbot refused to comply with these regulations, but had all his meals served in his chamber, absented himself from divine service, and continued to contract loans from divers persons of the county, and praying that the bishop of Salisbury should be ordered to reform these matters.[1] The abbot too, for his part, complained of the custodians. He accused them of holding costly feasts outside the monastery, but at its expense, and of wasting its goods in other ways, but it is evident that the chief and possibly the only real cause of his dissatisfaction was that they had deprived him of his separate chamber, and of his squire and two grooms and horses, to all of which, he said, an agreement made by the bishop of Winchester entitled him.[2] What truth there may have been in the abbot's account it is impossible to judge, but it seems unlikely that the custodians were committing the alleged wastes. The fact that the convent did not join with him in petitioning against the keepers; the desire of the latter for the intervention of the bishop of Salisbury, the diocesan; and the prominence which the abbot gave to his personal wrongs, all incline the reader to sympathize with the keepers.

It is not necessary, however, to decide between the parties to this quarrel, which was probably terminated by the resignation of the abbot in 1354.[3] To the historian, the documents concerning it are mainly valuable as proof of the activity of royal custodians. Unfortunately, no further records of the administration of custodians have so far been discovered, but the evidence here cited seems sufficient to show that their authority was great and that they were expected to use their wide powers, though what they actually did must remain, largely, a matter of conjecture. On the equally important question of the extent to which the religious houses benefited by the king's intervention, there is no direct evidence. Some slight indirect evidence of the advantages that might result from a period of custody may be found in a passage of the Evesham Chronicle. It is a eulogy of Abbot Henry, who ruled the monastery from 1256 to 1263, and in it the chronicler states that "although at the abbot's accession the monastery was in debt to the amount of fourteen hundred marks, within a short time the abbot entirely satisfied all the

[1] *Ancient Petitions*, 10471. [2] *Ibid.* 10470.
[3] *Cal. Pat. Rolls*, 1354–58, p. 73.

creditors and meanwhile, by the grace of God, lived honourably without a new loan".[1] Here all the praise for the monastery's recovery is given to the abbot, but, in 1259, he and his convent obtained from the king a grant of protection, and the appointment of two custodians, one of them a monk of the house, "to keep the said abbey and its issues, for the discharge of its debts, and to render account yearly to the abbot and convent, with someone deputed on behalf of the king to audit the account".[2] There is no means of discovering what success attended this arrangement, or how long it endured, but it seems likely that the speedy payment of the abbot's debts may be due, in part at least, to the assistance rendered by the keepers. But the most important indication that the administration by royally appointed custodians was not without effect comes from the frequency with which this form of assistance was requested. That the monasteries should have continued to petition the king for his special protection and the appointment of custodians, had these measures been altogether fruitless, is most unlikely. The grant of special protection would in itself be an important aid towards a monastery's recovery, but this could be, and from time to time was, obtained when no custodians were appointed; and when the monks asked also that keepers of their monastery should be assigned, one must conclude that they wished to procure the help which such men could give.

In issuing his commissions for the monasteries the king was, as we have seen, acting in his capacity of patron, and the protection and assistance which he thus afforded to houses of royal foundation in times of their most serious distress should be remembered as to some extent offsetting the king's demands for corrodies and other exactions, which are often emphasized when the difficulties of monastic finance are discussed. But, though he might be merely exercising the rights, or fulfilling the duties of a patron, the fact remained that he was the king, and, in practice, the two capacities could not be kept strictly separate. At the time the monasteries no doubt benefited by being under the protection of the most powerful patron in the land, but in admitting and even seeking the king's intervention, they were indirectly preparing the way for that exercise of royal authority by which eventually the monasteries were dissolved.

[1] *Chron. Abbatiae de Evesham*, p. 280. [2] *Cal. Pat. Rolls*, 1258–66, p. 58.

CHAPTER II

ROYAL VISITATIONS OF HOSPITALS AND FREE CHAPELS

In the affairs of the monasteries which have been discussed in the last chapter, the king's authority was largely restricted to temporal matters and was in all cases limited by the rights of the bishops and of the religious orders to which the monasteries belonged. But there were certain ecclesiastical foundations over which the power of the crown was practically absolute. These were those collegiate churches which were known as "royal free chapels", and the hospitals which either owed their establishment to some king of England or had acquired the status of royal foundations through their patronage having passed to the crown by escheat or gift. These were held to be exempt from the jurisdiction of their diocesans, and subject only to the authority of those who were set over them by the crown. Their immunity from episcopal control was not indeed quietly conceded by the church; bishops and archbishops repeatedly endeavoured to exercise in them the rights of visitors, but such attempts almost invariably aroused strenuous opposition both from the crown and from the ecclesiastics who were actually in possession and, consequently, the bishops were seldom successful. The most important conflicts over this right belong, however, to the half century preceding our period, and by the beginning of Edward III's reign the bishops had, tacitly at least, acknowledged the exemption of these houses. During the time here considered, we rarely meet with attempts to subject a house of this kind to episcopal control. Grandisson indeed, to judge from many documents in his register, seems to have had much difficulty in maintaining the exemption of Bosham, of which he held the deanery, against the bishops of Chichester and archbishops of Canterbury. This chapel was in a peculiar if not a unique position; for though it was termed a royal free chapel, the deanery belonged by a grant of Edward I to the bishop of Exeter for the time being, and the rights of visitation there seem to have been less clearly defined than in the case of other free chapels.

Another instance occurred in 1355, when the king commissioned the prior of Llanthony by Gloucester and William de Chiltenham to find by inquisition in the county of Gloucester to whom the right of visitation in the hospital of St Bartholomew, Gloucester, belonged. The reason given for this enquiry was that the king had appointed a commission of visitation of the hospital and afterwards petition was made to him "on behalf of R[eynold] bishop of Worcester, to revoke such commission on the ground that the bishop has ever had the office of visitation in that hospital and the king has never intermeddled therein from the time of the foundation".[1] At the inquisition held in obedience to this command the jurors said that the hospital had the title of a royal foundation by virtue of certain grants made to it by Henry III, but that the right of visitation in it belonged to the bishop of Worcester, but by what right they knew not.[2] In spite of this verdict, however, the king continued to issue commissions for the visitation of St Bartholomew's,[3] and we hear no more of the bishop's claim.

But with few exceptions the free chapels and hospitals of royal foundation were, during our period, left entirely under the control of the crown. The manner in which this control was exercised, and its effect on the free chapels and hospitals, offer many interesting parallels and contrasts both to the episcopal procedure and to the means employed by the crown for the relief of the monasteries.

Subjection to the crown instead of to the diocesan meant that most, if not all, cases concerning it would be determined according to the rules of the lay courts instead of according to the usage of the church, but the house was not altogether withdrawn from the control of ecclesiastical persons, for hospitals and free chapels in the patronage of the king were in fact under the supervision of the chancellor of England, who, until 1340, was always a cleric and usually a bishop, and even after that date lay chancellors were extremely rare. The chancellor's rights over such houses were strictly maintained against other officials of the

[1] *Cal. Pat. Rolls*, 1354–58, p. 291. [2] Dugdale, *Monasticon*, VII, p. 689.
[3] *Cal. Pat. Rolls*, 1358–61, pp. 74, 224.

crown. Thus, in 1359, when the escheator in the county of Huntingdon had seized into the king's hand the hospital of St Margaret without Huntingdon, because by inquisition of office he had found that the master had failed to maintain a chaplain for the daily celebration of divine service and to do other works of piety established there, he was ordered to restore the hospital with its lands, rents and other possessions to the master because the correction of hospitals and all chapels which were of the king's patronage belonged to the chancellor of England and to no other minister.[1]

The correction of houses of the class here referred to was usually effected by means of a visitation, but how often they were undertaken is uncertain. According to Miss Clay, the author of our only monograph on English medieval hospitals, "the patron or his agents, were supposed to inspect the premises, accounts etc., yearly",[2] but no authority is cited in support of this statement, and Miss Clay goes on to observe that "This civil visitation was frequently neglected, especially that of the chancellor on behalf of the Crown. Abuses were apt to accumulate until a royal commission of enquiry and reformation became obligatory".[3] Some hospitals which were of the patronage of towns, such as Bridport, were certainly visited annually,[4] the rule being, perhaps, a result of the annual change of officials of the borough, but this does not prove that all patrons were expected to do likewise, and I have found no indications of such a duty with regard to any hospitals which were not under the control of the towns. Occasionally, indeed, the Patent and Close Rolls contain traces of visitations for which no commissions are extant, and it is therefore just possible that the ordinary visitations, which Miss Clay believes should have taken place annually, were held by virtue of commissions of which no record has survived. But evidence of visitations under royal authority, for the holding of which no order can now be found, occur so seldom that it seems much more likely that the recording of the orders for them was accidentally omitted than that they belong to a class for which the commissions were not enrolled. If this view is correct, we

[1] *Cal. Close Rolls*, 1354–60, p. 556.
[2] R. M. Clay, *The Mediaeval Hospitals of England*, p. 138.
[3] *Ibid.* [4] *Ibid.*

may regard the commissions which the Patent Rolls contain as practically the total number that were issued, and an examination of these shows that whatever may have been the theory as to the frequency of visitations, both the hospitals and the collegiate churches that were under the chancellor's jurisdiction were seldom, if ever, troubled by the visitors so long as they remained of good report.

In this respect, the methods employed by the crown seem to have differed widely from those of the bishops. A bishop usually endeavoured to visit the parishes and religious houses of his see at least once during his episcopate, beginning this task as soon as possible after his consecration, and the more conscientious tried to visit at regular intervals.[1] To perform this task, the bishop generally made a tour through his diocese, or some part of it, during which almost every house under his jurisdiction would be visited, irrespective of its reputed condition. The crown, on the other hand, to judge from the extant records, seems to have interfered only when complaints concerning the spiritual or temporal state of a house had reached the king. A separate writ, commanding certain persons to make the visitation, and often explaining in some detail what faults required correction, appears to have been issued in almost every case; instances of a single commission being appointed to visit more than one house do, indeed, occur, but they are extremely rare; that which concerned the largest number of houses being a writ of 1368, ordering five persons to visit the king's free chapels of Bridgnorth, Stafford, Tettenhall, and St Mary, Shrewsbury, in all of which serious defects were alleged to exist.[2]

Another respect in which a royal visitation differed from that of a bishop was in the personnel of the visitors. The diocesan endeavoured to conduct his visitations in person, though, of course, attended by some of his household, who assisted him in the examination of the house and its members, and when this was impossible he entrusted the task to his commissaries, who were usually clerks of his household, and in all cases those who took part in episcopal visitations were ecclesiastics. The chancel-

[1] C. R. Cheney, *Episcopal Visitation of Monasteries in the thirteenth century*, pp. 123, 124.

[2] *Cal. Pat. Rolls*, 1367–70, p. 142.

lor could, of course, visit in person, and appears to have done so occasionally when the state of a London house required investigation. Thus, two of the visitations for which no commissions have survived, one of St Martin's le Grand, and the other of the hospital of St Katharine by the Tower, were held by the chancellor,[1] and his name also appears in one of the commissions for visiting the former house.[2] But the ordinary duties of his office naturally precluded his travelling about the country for the purpose of holding visitations. Except in the cases just mentioned, the duty was therefore invariably entrusted to a commission, comprising at least two and often as many as five or six men. Such a commission, in its personnel, resembled that which the king appointed to assist an impoverished monastery rather than that which a bishop would have sent in his stead for the purpose of visitation. Ecclesiastics and laymen seem to have been appointed in approximately equal numbers. Among the latter class we find no great nobles, but members of the local gentry frequently served on these commissions, sometimes for no apparent reason, and sometimes on account of their tenure of some office in the shire, as when Hugh de Moriceby, sheriff of Cumberland, was named among the visitors of the hospital of St Nicholas, Carlisle.[3] Moreover, eminent lawyers like Robert Parving and William de Shareshull frequently served on commissions of this kind. Of the ecclesiastics to whom this duty was assigned, a very few were bishops. Only once during our period, in July 1340, was the diocesan appointed as a visitor, when the bishop of Carlisle was appointed with others to visit the hospital of St Nicholas in his city.[4] The only other houses directly under the crown which were visited by bishops were the free chapels of St Stephen, Westminster, and Bosham. A visitation of the first of these was committed to the bishop of Winchester in July 1376, and to the archbishop of Dublin and the bishop of Worcester in November of the same year.[5] When the free chapel of Bosham was in need of reform the bishop of Exeter for the time being, who held the deanery, was usually directed to hold the visitation, in person or by deputy "in the

[1] *Cal. Close Rolls*, 1354–60, p. 65; *Cal. Pat. Rolls*, 1377–81, p. 507.
[2] *Cal. Pat. Rolls*, 1343–45, p. 185.
[3] *Ibid.* 1343–45, p. 575.
[4] *Ibid.* 1340–43, p. 89.
[5] *Ibid.* 1374–77, pp. 330, 410.

king's name and by his royal right",[1] and the documents preserved in the Exeter registers show that copies of the king's letters patent ordering the visitation had to be sent to the canons as part of the notice of the visitation which bishops were required to send.[2] The heads of monasteries in the neighbourhood of the houses to be visited were often among the commissioners. Thus the prior of St Mary's, Carlisle, appears in all of the four orders to visit the hospital of St Nicholas in that city;[3] in 1360, the abbots of Middleton and Bindon with Walter Waleys, a clerk, were appointed to visit the hospital of St John the Baptist at Dorchester;[4] while the abbots of Battle and of Robertsbridge were appointed in 1328 and 1341, respectively,[5] among the visitors of the free chapel of Hastings. The last case is remarkable, because after 1333, when Robertsbridge was allowed to appropriate the prebend of Salehurst belonging to the chapel, the abbot was one of the canons, having a stall in the choir, and a place in the chapter reserved to him.[6] But the majority of ecclesiastical visitors, and indeed the largest of any class of persons engaged in this work, were the clerks who served the king in the chancery or elsewhere, and who, doubtless, owed their appointment mainly to their position as civil servants, and especially to their connection with the chancery.

What considerations governed the choice of the visitors does not appear. The gentry and heads of religious houses who were employed usually belonged to the county in which the house to be visited was situated. The activities of the lawyers and king's clerks were naturally less restricted to particular localities, though it is interesting to see that in their case, too, local associations seem to have had some force. For example, Robert Parving, the great Cumberland lawyer, was concerned only with the northern houses of St Nicholas, Carlisle, and St Leonard, York.[7] A more important fact which appears from a close study of the names of the visitors is the repeated appointments of the same persons to

[1] *Cal. Pat. Rolls*, 1370–74, p. 315.
[2] *Reg. John de Grandisson*, ed. Hingeston-Randolph, part iii, pp. 1242, 1243.
[3] *Cal. Pat. Rolls*, 1334–38, p. 216; 1340–43, p. 89; 1343–45, p. 575; 1348–50, p. 176.
[4] *Ibid.* 1358–61, p. 326.
[5] *Ibid.* 1327–30, p. 354; 1340–43, p. 362.
[6] *Ibid.* 1330–34, p. 485.
[7] *Ibid.* 1340–43, pp. 89, 318.

deal with particular houses. Precisely the same group of commissioners was rarely reappointed, but when a house was visited several times, one or more persons who had previously visited it were likely to be found serving on each commission. For example, Henry de Edenstowe was four times appointed to visit the hospital of the Holy Innocents without Lincoln,[1] and Thomas de Sibthorp was a member of seven commissions which visited the same house.[2] This plan of committing the visitation of a hospital or free chapel to a group of men, some of whom had and some of whom had not previously visited it, would seem a most satisfactory arrangement. The presence of new commissioners might be expected to lessen the possibility of collusion between visitors and visitands, while the personal knowledge of the previous state of the house, which the members who had formerly enquired into it would possess, would give a certain continuity to the work, and enable a stricter watch to be kept over the conduct of those who had previously been found guilty of crimes or negligence. It is, however, impossible to say to what extent these advantages were actually secured; for, when more than two visitors had been appointed, it would appear that they were not all obliged to perform the duty in person. Letters patent by which the abbot of Fountains, John de Wodehouse, Peter de Richemond, Franco de Berneby and Thomas de Salcok were appointed to visit the hospitals of St John the Baptist and St Mary Magdalene at Ripon state that the task may be performed by the whole body, four, three, or two of them,[3] and the visitation was in fact conducted by four commissioners, all except Peter de Richemond;[4] and in 1340, when four persons were directed to visit St Nicholas's, Carlisle, we know that the visitation was actually conducted by two of them.[5]

A study of the commissions shows that there were practically two types of visitation; one, the most common type, which concerned both the temporal and spiritual welfare of the house,

[1] *Cal. Pat. Rolls*, 1340–43, pp. 97, 328, 444; 1343–45, p. 578.

[2] *Ibid.* 1334–38, pp. 143, 362; 1340–43, pp. 97, 328, 444; 1343–45, p. 422; 1345–48, p. 391.

[3] J. T. Fowler, *Memorials of Ripon*, I, p. 215. The *Calendar of Patent Rolls* omits the phrase "four three or two" and I am inclined to think that it might be found in other commissions if the originals instead of the Calendars had been consulted.

[4] *Ibid.* pp. 216, 217.

[5] *Cal. Pat. Rolls*, 1340–43, p. 120.

and the other, which was apparently intended to deal only with its temporal affairs, and amounted to little more than an enquiry into dilapidations. The second type, as it is the simpler and the less important, may be briefly examined first. It will be remembered that the king occasionally ordered an inquisition to be held when the head of a monastery of his patronage was thought to have dissipated its goods. Similar methods were employed when the heads of the king's hospitals and free chapels were accused of like offences, and, fortunately, the evidence as to what was done in these cases is much fuller than that which remains concerning the monasteries.

What seems at first a surprisingly large number of these enquiries with regard to dilapidations were ordered very soon after the appointment of a new head. At St Martin's le Grand there was an enquiry into the state of the house after the death or resignation of every dean who was suspected of having wasted its goods, and inquisitions were taken in similar circumstances at Wolverhampton, Wimborne Minster, and elsewhere. The commissioners who held these visitations, for so they are repeatedly styled, were required to find out what dilapidations had occurred in the time of the preceding dean and through his fault, and what it would cost to repair these defects. In obtaining this information they may have questioned the canons and vicars of the chapel, but it is clear that they were expected to depend mainly on the testimony of a jury of men of the county summoned for the purpose. The enquiry, moreover, was to be held in the presence of the new dean or his representatives, and of the executors of his predecessor's will, or of those into whose hands his goods had come, if they wished to attend. The presence of the latter would seem particularly important; for, if the visitors found that the chapel's possessions had been wasted during the late dean's tenure of office, the commissioners were to arrest his goods to the value of the estimated cost of the repairs. As a typical example of many such commissions, I quote the following, which was issued in 1369:

Commission to the abbots of Shrouesbery and Wenlok, Thomas de Ilston, Philip de Lutteleye and Thomas de Glasele to make a visitation of the king's free chapel of Bruggenorth and its members, in which, as the king is given to understand, there are many defects in the books, vestments and other ornaments, as well as in the manses, houses and other things pertaining to the deanery of the chapel in the county of Salop, since the time of Robert Ive, the last dean, in the presence of the king's clerk, Thomas de Brantyngham, the treasurer, to whom the king has now given the deanery, or his attorney deputed for this, as well as of the executors of the will of the said Robert Ive or of those in whose hands his goods now are; also to find whether the latter wasted the goods and possessions of the deanery and whether any of his goods should have been left to the present dean, by the name of implement, according to the statutes or customs of the chapel, and to have sufficient goods for the correction of the defects of the chapel arrested and kept safely until further order.[1]

The chapel that could thus be relieved of some, at least, of the natural consequences of a dean's misrule was in a fortunate position when compared with the monasteries whose heads would leave no goods of their own from which the defects they had caused might be repaired; and it may be partly owing to the practice I have just described that these chapels seem not to have become seriously burdened with debt.

There is no direct evidence of similar measures with regard to the hospitals of royal patronage, but in December 1349, a writ was issued commanding

John de Wodehouse, John Perot and Thomas de Santon to survey all defects in the king's hospital of St Nicholas by York, ...as it is reported that there are many such defects needing great repairs, and that divers alienations of the lands with which the hospital was founded have been made by wardens there to the prejudice of the king and of John de Ampleford, king's clerk, the present warden.[2]

And in February of the following year a commission with the same purport, but mentioning defects in the church and chancel, and in the books and ornaments, appears concerning St Leonard's, York.[3] Neither these commissions nor any other records now extant indicate how the defects were to be made good, but even if no immediate improvement could be brought about, it must have been greatly to the advantage of the incoming warden, whose predecessor had been dishonest or incompetent, to have the exact state of the house at the time of his admission put on

[1] *Cal. Pat. Rolls*, 1367–70, p. 347.
[2] *Ibid.* 1348–50, p. 458.
[3] *Ibid.* 1348–50, p. 518.

record, so that he should not be held responsible for what had happened before he became warden. Such investigations may therefore have been requested by the new heads of houses, and that this might be the case is shown by an inquisition which was held in 1323 concerning the state of the chapel in Tutbury Castle, at the end of which we read that this "inquisition was taken at the instigation of Jordan de Kynebell, the present chaplain of the castle".[1]

The new head of a hospital or collegiate church, the condition of which was unsatisfactory in other respects, might find a visitation, which should include enquiries as to the morals of the inmates, equally to his interests. It seems, therefore, not unlikely that the fairly frequent appearance of an order to visit a hospital within a few months of the warden's appointment may be due to the same cause. In May 1351, for example, Richard Creyk received a grant for life of the wardenship of the hospital of St John, Dorchester,[2] and in August of the same year a commission was appointed to visit the house "which is reported to be greatly decayed by misrule".[3] At this time, Richard Creyk cannot have been in possession of the house for more than three months, which would seem too short a time for his capacity as a warden to have become known, and it is more likely, therefore, that the complaint concerned his predecessors' misrule than his own faults, especially as he was not deprived of the mastership. This possible explanation should be borne in mind when the conduct of the masters in whose time visitations were held is considered. The visitations held in such circumstances formed, however, only a comparatively small proportion of the total number, and in the majority of cases a visitation was clearly intended to correct the faults of persons then belonging to the house.

How the need for such intervention was notified to the king I have not been able to discover. Members of the house who were dissatisfied with the conduct of the head or of their fellows may have petitioned for the king's interference, as did the monks of financially embarrassed monasteries; or some local official, such as the sheriff or escheator, may have drawn attention to the

[1] *Cal. of Inquisitions, Miscellaneous*, II, 747.
[2] *Cal. Pat. Rolls*, 1350–54, p. 69. [3] *Ibid.* 1350–54, p. 159.

decline of the house, which to judge from the detailed information which jurors were often able to give must have been a matter of common knowledge in the neighbourhood. But though we have no means of knowing the source of the information that correction was necessary, it seems certain that a visitation was rarely, if ever, ordered unless complaints regarding the condition of the house had been made. The commissions usually contained some such phrase as "on information that there are now many defects" or "complaint having reached the king's ears that there are defects". The letter to Thomas de Brantingham, bishop of Exeter, commanding him to visit the free chapel of Bosham, states that "the king has learned from many that there are many defects in it",[1] and, in 1362, a writ concerning the same chapel ordered John de Grandisson "to have the defects remedied that there be no more complaints made to the king in this behalf".[2]

The complaints which the king received must have concerned a wide variety of misdeeds as, in spite of a strong element of common form, we find in the portions of the writs which explain what faults would require special attention that many and very different causes made visitations necessary. Dilapidations appear to have been the most frequent source of trouble, the deans and canons of free chapels being most commonly accused of neglect of the books, vestments and church ornaments; and the masters of hospitals, of selling corrodies for their own profit, while both were constantly charged with having alienated or leased at too low a rate the lands of their houses.

Other offences, however, are often mentioned. In 1339, a visitation of the chapel in Windsor Castle was commanded,

> as it is reported that the warden and chaplains maintained there by the king's alms for the celebration of divine service have often absented themselves for a long time from the chapel without licence, whereby the divine worship which should be held there for the good estate of the king and the souls of his progenitors, kings of England, is withdrawn, and that many of the ornaments of the chapel are missing.[3]

In 1335, the commission appointing visitors for the hospital

[1] *Cal. Pat. Rolls*, 1370–74, p. 315. [2] *Ibid.* 1361–64, p. 210.
[3] *Ibid.* 1338–40, p. 354.

of St John the Baptist without the Eastgate of Oxford stated that it was "reported to be greatly decayed by misrule, and because some of the brothers, sisters and ministers show themselves disobedient and waste the goods of the hospital in divers ways, maintaining quarrels amongst themselves and leading lives otherwise dissolute".[1] But perhaps the most unsatisfactory state which any of these writs describes was the condition of the chapel of St Mary at Shrewsbury

concerning which complaints have reached the king's ears that there are defects in its ornaments and books, and that its officers and ministers neglect their duty by not officiating, although they receive their stipends, and that brawls arise among them, some of them leading a dissolute life, and that the dean makes new statutes in subversion of the rights and customs of the chapel, and introduces new customs, compelling the canons by threats and coercion to observe them, depriving and expelling them, and for a price bestowing their benefices on his accomplices.[2]

The writs themselves give many indications of what the commissioners were expected to do, and the information which may be derived from them is fortunately supplemented by the extant records of a number of visitations; for the commissioners were usually required to send into chancery a report of all that they had done. From a study of this material we learn that the procedure adopted by the commissioners was in many respects similar to that of a bishop or his commissaries when engaged in the like business. The royally appointed visitors apparently began their duties by ordering the sheriff to inform the visitands of their intention to visit the house on a specified day, but there is nothing to indicate that on their arrival the visitors required a certificate of this notice having been received, such as had always to be delivered to a bishop. Of the ceremonies that may have been observed when the commissioners arrived we have no record, nor is there any suggestion that a sermon was preached in their presence as it was at the beginning of an episcopal visitation. We hear, indeed, of a sermon preached at Bosham when John de Grandisson's commissaries visited that chapel,[3] but the observance of this form may well have been due to the

[1] *Cal. Pat. Rolls*, 1334–38, p. 211. [2] *Ibid.* 1327–30, p. 478.
[3] *Reg. John de Grandisson*, part iii, p. 1242.

fact that they were the representatives of a bishop. This point, however, must remain uncertain, as the records which the commissioners themselves sent into chancery were concerned only with the practical business of the visitation. These convey the impression that the commissioners set to work immediately, first requiring the head to show his title to the office and the rules and constitutions of the house, and then making enquiries as to its present state, both from the dean or warden and from the other inmates of the house. The account of the visitation of Bosham in 1363 suggests also that the visitors personally inspected the chapel with its books and other ornaments,[1] and this may well have been done in other cases when there had been complaints as to the condition of these things.

In one very important respect, however, the methods adopted by the crown officials differed from those of the bishops. The latter, to judge from the records they have left, seem in the great majority of cases to have obtained all their information from the written records of the visitands, such as the charters of their house and their account rolls, and from the verbal statements of the inmates of the house themselves. There is indeed one case which at first sight seems contrary to this practice. The vicar general of Richard Fleming, bishop of Lincoln, when ordering an enquiry as to the right of presentation to the hospital of SS. James and John, Brackley, wrote "we command...you to make diligent and faithful inquiry...by means of the most trustworthy rectors and vicars of churches who are neighbours of the same hospital, having the best knowledge of the premises and being present before you and sworn in form of law".[2] The return made in obedience to this injunction shows that twelve rectors and vicars, whose names with those of the parishes they served are all recorded, were interrogated. Here we have a group of men brought together for the purpose of giving evidence as was the jury of the royal inquisitions, but the matters about which they were questioned concerned only the patronage of the hospital, and it is further to be noted that no laymen were questioned.

In ordinary visitations the inmates of the house were not even

[1] *Reg. John de Grandisson*, part iii, p. 1244.
[2] *Visitations of Religious Houses in the diocese of Lincoln*, ed. A. Hamilton Thompson, I, p. 12.

examined on oath, though oaths could be, and often were, required in serious cases, but however grave the case might be, the bishops seem not to have empanelled a jury as to the temporal or spiritual state of a house from its neighbours. Indeed, to exclude the outside world from any participation in the visitation was a natural desire of the visitands, the Religious objecting even to the presence of secular clerks in the chapter-house during a visitation, and the bishops, while insisting upon taking with them the clerks who were necessary for the despatch of business, were also anxious to make the proceedings as private as possible.

No such regard for the privileges of the church or the feelings of the visitands was allowed to stand in the way of the royal commissioners when it was important to learn the truth, for their instructions often show that in the regular visitations information was to be obtained in the same way as in the enquiries which merely concerned dilapidations, that is, with the aid of a jury of men of the county. Thus the persons, who in 1351 were ordered to visit the hospital of St John the Baptist, Dorchester, were directed "to examine the warden, brothers and sisters, singly, and to find by jury of the county of Dorset the whole truth of the matter".[1] Sometimes, as in the case of St Bartholomew's, Gloucester, in 1345, we learn of the jury through the sheriff's being ordered to summon it as required by the visitors.[2]

The language of commissions like the one just cited for St John's, Dorchester, suggests that the commissioners were obliged to take the evidence of a jury. In other cases, the summoning of jurors of the neighbourhood would seem to have been left to their discretion, and was perhaps regarded as a last resort if the truth could not be elicited from the inmates of the house itself. This is the implication of phrases which frequently occur such as "to enquire, if necessary, by the oath of good men of the town of Hastynges".[3] Whether or not these words indicate a reluctance to expose the shortcomings of an ecclesiastical foundation to the criticism of its lay neighbours, the principle that a jury might be called was definitely established and there is abundant

[1] *Cal. Pat. Rolls*, 1350–54, p. 159.
[2] *Ibid.* 1343–45, p. 514.
[3] *Ibid.* 1361–64, p. 69.

evidence to prove that the information which the visitors collected was often obtained with its help.

It is not quite certain, however, whether the examination of the jury was, strictly speaking, a part of the visitation. A doubt as to this point is raised by the records concerning the visitations of the hospitals of St John the Baptist and St Mary Magdalene at Ripon. The commissioners, whenever they visited either of these hospitals, had a jury summoned before them to give evidence as to the state of the house; how far the masses and other works of piety which had been founded there were performed; and the character of the master and chaplains. But according to the reports that have come down to us in each case, the questioning of the jurors preceded the examination of the master and chaplains, and in at least one instance the latter is separated from the jurors' evidence under the heading "visitatio facta" in a way that implies that the examination of the jury was a ceremony apart from the visitation proper.[1] This view, however, is not supported by the records relating to the visitation of other houses, for in them the interrogating of the jury appears as a more integral part of the visitation itself.

What seems to have been the normal procedure is most clearly described in a record of a visitation of the hospital of St Nicholas, Carlisle, in 1340, which, contrary to the usual practice, was copied on to the patent roll of that year. According to this, the four commissioners, the bishop of Carlisle, the prior of St Mary's, Carlisle, Robert Parving and Robert de Eglesfield,

> Pursuant to the king's letters patent of 25 July, 14 Edward III, appointing them to make such visitation, the commissioners commanded the sheriff of Cumberland to summon a jury of twenty-four knights and others at the hospital on Tuesday before the Nativity of St Mary, and to warn the master, brethren and sisters to be there then to inform them touching some matters affecting the hospital. At which day came the said prior [of St Mary's, Carlisle] and Robert Parvyng, commissioners,

twelve jurors (whose names are given) and Thomas de Goldyngton, master of the hospital.[2] "The master is called on to produce

[1] *Memorials of Ripon*, I, p. 219.

[2] From the enquiry that followed it appears that there were no brethren or sisters in the hospital at the time.

any muniments, memoranda of the foundation, or rules relating to the hospital he may have." A long statement by Goldyngton explaining that the foundation charter and other muniments had been burned by the Scots, and giving his version of the recent history of the house follows, and then we read "And upon this the inquisition is taken, and the jurors say on oath that all these constitutions and many others used to be observed in the hospital".[1] But whether or not the questioning of the jury technically formed a part of the visitation, it is clear that the visitors made free and constant use of this means of discovering the state of the houses.

Probably the matters on which the testimony of a jury would be most valuable, and on which it was oftenest sought, concerned the granting away of the lands of the house or other wastes of its possessions. Men living in the neighbourhood of a parcel of land would almost certainly be aware if it changed hands; the tenants would be likely to talk of the event and the bailiff of the new lord would be seen about the premises. Neighbours might also be in a position to know what corrodies had been granted. But though the condition of the property of the house was the principal subject of enquiry from the jurors, questions were also asked with regard to the conduct of its inmates. Thus the men appointed, in July 1345, to visit the hospital of the Holy Innocents without Lincoln were directed "to make inquisition by oath of good men of the county of Lincoln touching the defects in the hospital, the bearing of the warden, brethren and sisters, all lapses from the rules and observances of the primeval foundation and all squandering of lands and possessions".[2]

Even with the aid of a jury it was not easy to learn the truth.[3] For on some occasions we find that the reports of two successive visitations are in direct contradiction. Thus the record of the inquisition concerning St Nicholas's, Carlisle, which was taken in 1335 gives a most favourable account of Thomas de Goldyngton who had then been master for nearly two years,[4] mentioning benefits that he had conferred on the house, and concluding "the

[1] *Cal. Pat. Rolls*, 1340–43, pp. 119–21.
[2] *Ibid.* 1343–45, p. 578.
[3] Professor Pollard remarks that "as late as the fifteenth century trial by jury was often a contest in perjury", *Wolsey*, p. 60.
[4] He was appointed Jan. 1334. *Cal. Pat. Rolls*, 1330–34, p. 491.

hospital has in no way deteriorated in his time, but is much improved by him".[1] But in the long report of the visitation of 1340, Goldyngton appears as a most unsuitable head.[2] Here there was a period of about five years between the two visitations and we may believe that Goldyngton began well and in time became less efficient or less honest, but in another instance of equally contradictory returns, the enquiries on which they were based were made within a few months of each other. In June 1327, an inquisition concerning the state of St Leonard's, Derby, was taken, at which it was disclosed that Roger de Luichirche, the master, had ejected a leper, and wasted the goods of the house.[3] Later in the same year, the house was visited by Adam le Brom, and another commissioner, who found its misfortunes to be mainly due to the misconduct of Roger de Duranthorpe, one of the infirm brethren whom they ordered the master to remove.[4] Nevertheless, the evidence of a jury must often have been of real value in itself; and to the inmates of the house the knowledge that the visitors would not be content with their statements alone must have greatly reduced the temptation to form a conspiracy of silence, such as frequently baffled the attempts of the episcopal visitors to learn the true state of a monastery.

The information which the visitors obtained both from the jury and from the members of the foundation was, as we have seen, sent into chancery, where it might form the basis of further orders concerning the house, such as writs to the escheator ordering him to seize into the king's hands lands which had been alienated without licence.[5] But the commissioners were expected to do far more than merely to collect information. For it was part of their duty as visitors to take immediate measures, based on what they had learned, for the reform of the house. The commissions usually contain a general order to the visitors to correct what they shall find amiss, but often the instructions given were much more detailed. In 1361, the visitors of the free chapel of Hastings were ordered "to correct all defects, punish

[1] *Cal. of Inquisitions, Miscellaneous*, II, 1456.
[2] *Cal. Pat. Rolls*, 1340–43, pp. 119 ff.
[3] *Cal. of Inquisitions, Miscellaneous*, II, 1005.
[4] *V.C.H. Derby*, II, pp. 84, 85.
[5] *Cal. Close Rolls*, 1330–33, pp. 434, 435.

delinquents and recover such liberties as they shall find to have been lost".[1] Those who visited St Bartholomew's, Gloucester, in 1358 were to

> seize into the king's hands all the corrodies to be taken out of the hospital, so granted to its destruction, and to order that the goods of the hospital be turned to the advantage of the hospital, that the brothers, sisters and poor therein be competently ministered therefrom in food and clothing and that the chantries be maintained, to find by inquisition and reform anything which they find to the prejudice of the hospital and chantries and to do all things that pertain to the office of visitors in this behalf.[2]

The directions which some of the commissioners received make it clear also that the powers entrusted to them were not always the same. This may be illustrated by two commissions for the visitation of the king's free chapel at Bridgnorth. In the first of these, issued in 1336, the visitors were directed "to reform where such visitation shows this to be necessary even if this should involve the removal or deprivation of some of the persons";[3] the second, which belongs to the year 1376, commanded the commissioners "to correct all defects found there and punish delinquents according to their deserts, without, however, proceeding so far as the removal of any person".[4] While a commission conferring powers between these two extremes is that concerning a visitation of the hospital of St John the Baptist, at Shrewsbury, which authorized the commissioners to "correct all defects which they find therein, punish delinquents, and do all things pertaining to the visitation of the hospital, the removal of the master or warden only excepted".[5]

Once, also, we find a distinction drawn between the powers of the lay and ecclesiastical members of the same commission. This occurs in letters patent of 1328, directing the abbot of Battle, Bartholomew de Burghersh, constable of Dover Castle and warden of the Cinque Ports, and Master John de Ufford to visit the king's free chapel of Hastings. The document, after men-

[1] *Cal. Pat. Rolls*, 1361–64, p. 69.
[2] *Ibid.* 1358–61, pp. 74, 75.
[3] *Ibid.* 1334–38, p. 365.
[4] *Ibid.* 1374–77, pp. 323, 324.
[5] *Ibid.* 1374–77, p. 312.

tioning the dilapidations and crimes of which the king had heard, ordered the commissioners

to visit the dean, canons residentiary, vicars and other ministers of the said chapel, and survey its condition and that of its books and ornaments, informing themselves, both by personal examination and inquisition on oath of the said ministers and men of those parts, touching the defects and excesses aforesaid, to repair the one and correct the other, and punish offenders according to the ordinances and statutes of the chapel,...with a proviso that the said warden meddle not with the correction of souls.[1]

Whether the difference here expressed, between the functions of the lay and clerical visitors, was in fact observed elsewhere there is, at present, no means of deciding. Such a distinction might be expected in view of the church's opposition to the interference of laymen in matters of ecclesiastical discipline, but on the other hand, it is possible that where the king was supreme, laymen who visited in his name may have exercised jurisdiction which was elsewhere reserved to members of the clergy. At any rate, I have found no other indication of the restriction of a lay visitor's authority.

Of the measures which the visitors actually took we know far less than could be desired, but enough evidence is extant to show that their coming might reasonably be dreaded by the guilty. In the case of the hospitals, the punishments to be inflicted were usually laid down in the rule. Thus we read that at St Nicholas's, Carlisle,

the brethren and sisters should be obedient to the precepts of the master or his vicegerent in all things lawful and honest, and any brother or sister found refractory or disobedient, for the first offence should lose his or her livery, and be admonished, for the second should lose the two next liveries and be admonished to amend, otherwise on the third offence he or she should be expelled from the cloister and be entirely deprived of his or her corrody without hope of return.[2]

The practice of reserving ejection from the house as a final punishment to be inflicted only after a third offence seems to have been followed also with regard to the vicars of the free chapels. For in 1319, when five of the vicars of Hastings were

[1] *Cal. Pat. Rolls*, 1327–30, p. 354. [2] *Ibid.* 1340–43, p. 120.

convicted of having stolen money and ornaments belonging to the chapel, four were removed, but the fifth was allowed to remain as this was not his third offence.[1] Probably the visitors from time to time ordered the infliction of the lesser penalties which the rule allowed, but we hear most concerning their action in really serious cases. The master of the hospital of St Katharine by the Tower of London was deprived after a visitation early in Edward III's reign,[2] and the appointments of new masters which occur almost immediately after the visitations of other houses suggest that other wardens also were removed or induced to resign.

If the visitors did not at once remove an unsatisfactory head, they might refer his case to a higher authority and make temporary provision for the rule of his house until the case should have been decided. Thus at the end of the long account of the proceedings at St Nicholas's, Carlisle, in 1340, we read

> the master has been told to be before the king in his chancery at Westminster in fifteen days of Michaelmas, to abide the order of the council herein, and the common seal has been taken from the master and corrody holders to be delivered to the custody of the prior of Carlisle, under the seal of the said master, until the king by his council see fit to order otherwise.[3]

Mention has already been made of the vicars of Hastings who were removed at the visitation of 1319, and at a subsequent visitation of the same house, in 1345, "four vicars were ejected for continuing to keep concubines in spite of the dean's prohibition".[4] Occasionally, too, the brethren of hospitals lost their places in consequence of crimes which were disclosed at a visitation. One particularly interesting case of this kind concerns a brother of St Leonard's, Derby, and has been related in some detail in the Victoria County History's account of that house. A commission was appointed to visit St Leonard's in 1327, and, soon after, the three visitors repaired to the house, where they examined the warden and four brethren, two able-bodied and two infirm. The warden, after answering the customary questions as to his appointment and the rules of the house, stated that

[1] *V.C.H. Sussex*, II, p. 115.
[2] *Cal. Close Rolls*, 1333–37, pp. 47, 48.
[3] *Cal. Pat. Rolls*, 1340–43, p. 123. [4] *V.C.H. Sussex*, II, p. 116.

Roger de Duranthorpe, one of the infirm brethren,[1] had carried off the foundation charter and the common seal without leave of the warden and brethren, and had involved the house by giving many bonds sealed with the same seal for various sums of money to certain persons. The warden further accused him of having sold wool and lambs belonging to the stock of the hospital, the proceeds of which sales were wasted and expended by Roger on bailiffs and others to take his part against the warden. The other brethren were interrogated singly and their statements agreed in all points with the warden's. Roger de Duranthorpe was then sworn. He acknowledged that he had the charter and seal, but said they were in safe custody in the town of Derby. He was then ordered to fetch them, and promising faithfully to do so, went out for that purpose, the commissioners, apparently, awaiting his return. When at length he reappeared, he said that he had changed his mind, and refused to give up the seal and charter though commanded to do so in the king's name and by his oath of obedience; nor would he answer their questions. The visitors, therefore, gave sentence that he should be ejected from the house and ordered the master no longer to allow him to remain there.[2]

If Duranthorpe was really responsible for the crimes with which he was charged it may be easily imagined how greatly his removal might improve the state of the house. Judging from the comparatively few records of royal visitations that have come down to us, it would seem that the removal of unsuitable members of the community was one of the most common methods adopted by the visitors for the relief of a house. This power must have made the correction of the hospitals and free chapels an easier task than the reform, from outside, of the monasteries. For a monk could not be turned out into the world. Whatever his offences, he remained a monk, and throughout his life provision had to be made for him either in his own monastery or in some other house of his order. Thus there was always the possibility of his causing dissensions or finding some means of avenging himself on those who were responsible for his punish-

[1] The infirm brethren were lepers, who, at this, as at other houses, were allowed by the rule a large share in the management of its affairs. This circumstance probably accounts for Roger's being able to sell the goods of the house. See *Cal. of Inquisitions, Miscellaneous*, II, 1005.

[2] *V.C.H. Derby*, II, pp. 84, 85.

ment. Moreover, as we have seen in the last chapter, the head of a monastery who had been deprived very often appealed to the pope, thereby not infrequently securing his restoration to authority, but in any event involving his house in great expense. The danger of similar evils was not entirely absent from the hospitals and free chapels, for a deprived head might bring an action against his successor. It would, however, be a suit not in the ecclesiastical, but in the civil court, and expensive as that might be, it must have cost far less than an appeal to Rome. The task of effecting permanent improvement in the state of these houses was, however, almost impossible. In the collegiate churches the deans and canons were usually non-resident pluralists who took little interest in their benefices except as sources of revenue. Some indeed, like Wykeham when he was dean of St Martin's le Grand, conferred great benefits on their churches, but more left them in no better if not in a positively worse condition than when they took office. And the same may be said of the masters of most of the hospitals. These difficulties, however, were not due to the system of visitation, but to the almost universal medieval practice of paying the civil servants and providing for the younger members of great families by means of ecclesiastical preferment. The same difficulties therefore confronted the episcopal visitors, and it does not appear that they were more successful in overcoming them.

There were no doubt grave disadvantages in both systems. The chancellor's practice of leaving houses unvisited for long periods until offences had accumulated must, in many cases, have led to a relaxation of discipline, but at least it spared the houses the frequent payment of procurations which the smaller houses, visited by the bishops, found a serious burden, and which must have seemed to them a needless expense when there was little or nothing to reform. Moreover, when the crown did intervene, the enquiries made appear to have been more searching, and the methods adopted for the improvement of the house more drastic, than those of the bishops. It must, therefore, be concluded that in the matter of external supervision, the hospitals and free chapels which were directly under the crown were certainly not in a worse state than those houses in whose affairs only the church was concerned.

CHAPTER III

ALIENATIONS IN MORTMAIN

THE material on which the two foregoing chapters have been based we owe largely to efforts on behalf of the crown to prevent the dissipation of property belonging to certain religious houses. But however desirous the rulers of the state might be that the church should not lose or waste the possessions which it already held, they were much more anxious to control its acquisitions of fresh property. This they sought to do by means of Edward I's famous Statute of Mortmain.

Whatever medieval men may have thought of this statute, the modern student of ecclesiastical history cannot fail to be grateful for it, since it resulted in the keeping of a large number of records, enrolled on the Patent Rolls, which furnish valuable evidence on several aspects of the life of the church. These records must now be considered.

But first, something should be said with regard to the Statute of Mortmain itself, and the extent to which it was enforced. As is well known, the Statute of Mortmain expressly forbade the alienation of land or rent to the church, declaring that breaches of this law should be punished by forfeiture of the alienated property to the lord of whom it was held; and if he failed to take possession, the right of entering passed to the lord next above him and so, successively, to each lord until it reached the king. These provisions seem never to have been strictly enforced; large amounts of land and rent continued to be acquired by the church, and, therefore, the statute has generally been regarded as ineffective. Thus Tout in summarizing its consequences wrote:

> The statute of Mortmain hardly stayed the creation of fresh monasteries and colleges, or the further endowment of old ones. All that was necessary for the pious founder was to obtain a royal dispensation from the operation of the statute. There was little need to fear that the new law would stand in the way of the power of the ecclesiastical estate.[1]

[1] T. F. Tout, *The Political History of England*, 1216–1377, p. 152.

The first two of these statements are undeniable, and if the statute is judged solely by its success in preventing the church's acquisition of property it will be found to have been almost useless, but, although its avowed purpose was not fulfilled, it nevertheless led to important results affecting the relations of church and state. For, although as soon as the statute was promulgated, licences suspending its operation in particular cases began to be issued, the government seems to have determined that no amount of land or rent, however small, should pass into mortmain without the king's assent. Indeed it might be said that the statute was interpreted to mean that no property should be alienated in mortmain unless the king's licence had been obtained; and that the law in this modified form was rigorously enforced, there is, as will be shown later, abundant evidence to prove. Thus the statute secured to the state the important advantage of subjecting all grants to the church to strict royal control.

The obtaining of a royal licence, moreover, was not a simple matter. The man who wished to confer land or rent on the church had to petition the king for his assent to the grant, and the assent would not be given immediately. When such a petition was received, the usual procedure was to send a writ to the escheator of the county, where the property in question lay, directing him to hold an inquisition ad quod damnum—that is, to find out by the sworn testimony of neighbours, called together for the purpose, what was the yearly value of the property, of whom it was held, and what losses the king would sustain if it came into the hands of the church. After the information thus obtained had been returned into chancery, the question of the issue of the licence for the alienation in mortmain would have to be considered.[1] I know of no instance in which such a licence was refused, but this does not prove that they were always granted, as a careful record of all the licences that were issued would necessarily be kept, while there would be small advantage in preserving petitions which had not been granted. But even if all the licences that were asked for were issued, the requirement that they must be obtained was not only an extension of the

[1] This account of the procedure is based on a comparison of the Inquisitions Ad Quod Damnum and the Patent Rolls.

royal authority over the affairs of the church, but a means of securing some material advantage to the crown. This profit came from the fines which were usually exacted in payment for the licences.

Some difficult questions are raised by these fines. It is certain that they were often far more than payments for the expenses involved in taking the necessary inquisition and issuing the licence, but the extent to which they may be regarded as amounting, in theory or in practice, to what might be considered adequate compensation for the losses which the king would suffer, cannot be determined. They seem to have borne no fixed proportion to the value of the alienated property, and, though the cause of their variations may often be guessed, there is no certain means of discovering them. The differences in the amounts charged may be well illustrated by a comparison of the fines demanded for two licences by which chantries were to be established at Kingston upon Hull. These licences were issued about the same time, and concerned grants of the same value, six marks of rent; yet for the first, a fine of six marks was required, while for the second, only twenty shillings was paid.[1] In this case the marked difference was probably due to the fact that the second licence was granted at the instance of William de la Pole, upon whom the king, at that time, depended for financial support.

The necessity or the desire of showing favour to particular individuals may well account for many surprisingly small fines, and for some of the entire omissions of any charge, which also not infrequently occur. In the licences for which no fine was to be paid, the reason for the king's generosity is occasionally expressed, and it is pleasing to find that such favours seem, sometimes, to have been genuine marks of gratitude towards comparatively humble persons. For instance, in 1332, the king issued a "Licence for the alienation in mortmain by Robert de Bardelby, king's clerk, canon of Holy Trinity Church, Chichester, to the dean and chapter of the said church, of 20*s*. in rent in Chichester, for the celebration of his anniversary every year with the masses and other services of the dead required on days of anniversary", and it is added that "This licence is granted for

[1] *Cal. Pat. Rolls*, 1327–30, p. 304.

laudable service in the Chancery in the reign of Edward I, Edward II, and the present king, discharged at great cost to himself".[1]

In some cases also the king's good will towards the ecclesiastics who were to benefit by an alienation may have lessened the amount of the fine exacted, and the degree of probability of the property's falling into the king's hands may also have affected the payment for the licence.

All these possibilities must be remembered when one is studying the fines, but the chief difficulty—one which, at present, seems insurmountable—in the way of deciding whether the fines may be regarded as in any way compensating for the king's losses by alienations, is that it is generally uncertain to what extent an alienation in mortmain was actually to the king's prejudice. For it must be borne in mind that an alienation of land in mortmain, though it would deprive the overlord of the fine which was payable when each new tenant took up the holding, did not necessarily diminish the annual profits which he was accustomed to receive. Thus in 1349, the king granted to John de Scarle, king's clerk, parson of the church of St Thomas, Winchelsea,

> to which church as yet no certain manse or place for the inhabitation of the rector pertains, a messuage with appurtenances..., which has come into the king's hands as an escheat...to make a rectory thereof, he rendering at the exchequer yearly by the hands of the bailiff of that town such farm as used to be rendered before the messuage came into the king's hands and saying daily in his parochial mass a special collect for the king's good estate and for his soul when he is no more.[2]

Had the king not made this grant, some lay tenant would, almost certainly, have obtained the messuage for a like farm, so that by the alienation he sacrificed no material advantage except his right to the gersum, and the possibility of increasing the farm when the messuage was regranted at some future time, while he at once gained the spiritual benefit of the daily collect.

Moreover, though a piece of property when it had been alienated in mortmain would not again escheat to the crown or be charged with reliefs, it would, if it belonged to a monastery, collegiate church, or bishopric, be taken into the king's hands

[1] *Cal. Pat. Rolls*, 1330–34, p. 254. [2] *Ibid.* 1348–50, p. 369.

during every voidance. In the period with which this study deals, voidances of bishoprics or monasteries were, as a rule, short, but they were often frequent, and, therefore, in some cases at least, the king may have derived as much profit from a piece of land after it had passed into mortmain as it would have yielded to him had it remained in the possession of lay tenants.

But whether the fine was levied in accordance with any understood principle, or whether it was merely the largest sum that the petitioner for the licence seemed likely to pay, the sums paid were considerable, often amounting to two or three times the annual value of the property concerned. For example, in 1359, ten pounds were paid for a licence to grant a toft and six marks of rent to a chaplain, and in 1368, twenty pounds were required for a licence to grant eight marks of rent in mortmain.[1] From this it seems likely that when the king allowed property to be alienated in mortmain, he might be impoverishing his heirs, but for himself he was probably securing as much revenue as the property would have yielded to the crown during his lifetime.

It was probably in order to lessen the amount paid as fines that many ecclesiastical corporations obtained from the king licences to acquire land and rent in mortmain up to a specified amount, usually ten or twenty pounds. Such a licence would be granted in return for a fine, or sometimes, apparently, merely through the king's favour,[2] and the corporation which possessed it need pay no further fine on entering into possession of any amount of land or rent up to the prescribed value, though a further fine would be paid if the property acquired was found to be worth more than the original general licence allowed. Thus in 1363, the prior and convent of Royston obtained a licence to receive in mortmain from Thomas Palfreyman of Royston, chaplain, a messuage and forty acres of land, one acre of meadow,

[1] *Cal. Pat. Rolls*, 1358–61, p. 214; 1367–70, p. 169.

[2] In 1375, the prior and convent of Great Malvern were given a licence to acquire land and rent not held in chief to the yearly value of twenty pounds, because "Thomas Mawardyn, who while he was secular was a valiant knight and did the king praiseworthy service, has now entered religion and dwells as a monk professed in the priory". (*Cal. Pat. Rolls*, 1374–77, p. 82.) How great a benefit the former knight thus conferred on the house is apparent when we observe that eleven years earlier, the canons of St Germain in Cornwall paid eighty pounds for an identical privilege. (*Ibid.* 1364–67, p. 4.)

forty acres of pasture and one acre of wood, of the value of 11*s.* 5*d.* yearly; "to hold in full satisfaction of 100*s.* yearly of land and rent which they have the king's licence to acquire. By fine of 10*s.* because the tenements acquired exceed the value of the tenements contained in the licence".[1]

The fact that the value of this land exceeded that specified in the licence had probably become known through the inquisition ad quod damnum, for a general licence did not exempt the ecclesiastics who had procured it from the necessity of seeking a licence for the acquisition of each parcel of land or rent towards the specified amount, and of waiting until the customary inquisitions ad quod damnum had been taken before entering into possession. This is shown by the very frequent occurrence of such clauses as "to hold in satisfaction of a hundred shillings of the ten pounds yearly of land and rent which they have the king's licence to acquire". Moreover, the words "provided that inquisitions be first taken" occur not infrequently in the general licences, and instances of punishments for failure to observe this rule may be cited. The Patent Rolls of 1371 contain a

Pardon, for 20*s.* paid to the king by the prior and convent of Brymmore, to them of the trespass of John, late prior of Brymmore, in acquiring in mortmain [certain messuages, land and rent] without inquisition or other process in Chancery, which messuages, land and rent are not held of the king and are of the yearly value of 18*s.* 8*d.*...; and restitution of the premises to them in satisfaction of 40*s.* of the 10 marks yearly of land and rent which they had the king's licence to acquire.[2]

Similarly, in 1364, the abbot of Dieulacres petitioned the king for restoration to him and his convent of messuages and land, valued at 20*s.* yearly, "which have been taken into the king's hand because acquired after the date of the licence...[to acquire land and rent to the yearly value of ten pounds] and entered into without any inquisition or other process in the Chancery made".[3]

These and similar records suggest that the legal punishment for entering into possession before the requisite inquisition had been taken was the same as that for acquiring land or rent in mortmain without any licence, forfeiture to the crown of the

[1] *Cal. Pat. Rolls*, 1361–64, p. 303.
[2] *Ibid.* 1370–74, p. 53.
[3] *Ibid.* 1364–67, p. 33.

property concerned. Those who had incurred this penalty for either offence were often able, on payment of a fine, to secure a pardon and restitution of the forfeited property, but it was by no means certain that such a trespass would be pardoned. In 1375, there was issued a

> Grant for life to the king's servant, Richard Alban, of a messuage with 2 houses built thereon in Orpyngton, co. Kent, late of Nicholas de Yistele, late parson of the church of Orpyngton which are forfeit to the king because Robert de Ellebourne, late vicar of the said church, purchased them in mortmain from Nicholas without the king's licence as is found by inquisition,[1]

and the Patent Rolls record a number of similar grants.

More frequently, however, the king used property which had been so forfeited to endow ecclesiastical foundations in which he had a special interest. Of these, the one that received by far the largest share of such endowments during the reign of Edward III was the monastery of St Mary Graces by the Tower of London, which received altogether seven grants of such property amounting in value to approximately 92 marks. The number of gifts of this kind bestowed on this monastery was probably due to its situation in London, as well as to the fact that it had been founded by Edward III himself, for most of the property lay in London, and had been bequeathed in mortmain without the king's licence to various churches of the city for chantries and alms—the revenues of sixteen chantries being thus absorbed. In some cases the duty of praying and celebrating masses for the souls of the original grantors was imposed upon the monks,[2] but in other instances, no duties seem to have been attached to the holding of the property.[3]

How it happened that some ecclesiastics were able to obtain pardons while others had to forfeit their illegally acquired possessions we have no means of knowing. But it is interesting to observe that during the period from February 1371 to January 1377, when a lay chancellor was in power, the number of forfeitures considerably increased. During the years 1365 to 1371, the Patent Rolls mention fifteen alienations in mortmain which had been made without licence. In eleven of these cases the

[1] *Cal. Pat. Rolls*, 1374–77, p. 126.
[2] *Ibid.* 1367–70, pp. 323–4.
[3] *Ibid.* 1374–77, p. 429.

offenders were pardoned and allowed to retain what they had acquired. In two cases they were deprived of the property which the king granted in mortmain to other ecclesiastics, and in two cases the forfeited possessions were granted, not in mortmain, but to individuals. One of the last-mentioned grants, however, would seem to have been only part of a device, of which the chancery may or may not have been aware at the time, for restoring the property to the deprived monastery. For by letters patent dated June 8, 1367, a tenement, and the advowson of the church of St Swithin, London, which the king recovered against the prior and convent of Tortington because they had been put in mortmain without licence, were granted to Richard, earl of Arundel, and a licence of June 21, in the same year, permitted the earl to grant the tenement and advowson to the priory.[1] In the years 1371–77, twenty-five alienations in mortmain without licence are recorded, and for only twelve of these were pardons obtained. The rest were forfeit; in three cases the property being bestowed on other ecclesiastical foundations, and in ten being granted to individuals, most of whom were laymen and servants of the king.

Of the land and rent which came into the king's hands because it had been acquired in mortmain without licence, bequests for pious objects seemed to have formed a large proportion. Some ecclesiastics were cautious, and hastened to obtain the king's assent to their acquisition of the property so left to them before entering into possession. Thus in 1371, letters patent were issued granting

> Licence, for ten marks paid in the hanaper by the prior of St Denys by Suthampton, for him and his convent to enter into a messuage in Suthampton...of the yearly value of 26*s.* 8*d.*...which Roger Haywode bequeathed to them in mortmain in aid of the sustenance of a canon as chaplain to celebrate divine service daily in the conventual church for his soul and the souls of all the faithful departed; the prior having shewed the king that they dared not enter therein without his licence.[2]

The canons of this priory were aliens and for that reason they may have found it particularly important to observe all the required legal forms, but the experience of many who were not aliens proves that the convent's fears were well founded.

[1] *Cal. Pat. Rolls,* 1364–67, p. 409.   [2] *Ibid.* 1370–74, p. 115.

The frequent notices of forfeitures furnish in themselves strong evidence of the strictness with which the Statute of Mortmain was enforced, and they are not the only indications of the care that was taken to see that the law was observed. In 1368, William de Catesby, John de Catesby and William Chaumberleyn were commissioned "to find by inquisition... what lands the prior and convent of Kenelworth acquired in mortmain in the county of Warwick without the king's licence".[1] Another enquiry which was made when an alienation without licence was suspected resulted in the issue of the following document, which I quote in full on account of its exceptional interest:

Whereas lately, on presentation made before the king that the prior of Gysburn acquired in mortmain without the king's licence a plot of land, meadow and pasture...from John de Fauconbergge, who held it in chief, the king had the said plot taken into his hand, and afterwards the prior came before the king and asserted that neither he nor his predecessors acquired the plot; and whereas it was found by the inquisition on which he put himself that the prior did not acquire the plot but that the said John granted to Robert, prior of Gysburn, and the convent of that place that they might cut down and carry away at their pleasure all the wood then growing, or thenceforth to grow, in a close called 'Swatyheved' in Gysburn, enclosed by a dyke and a stream called 'Swynstybek', and that they might have common of pasture for their cattle in the said close, and take or do all things which could turn to their profit, and granted that neither he nor his heirs would depasture the said close with their cattle, nor take any profit of the wood or pasture, or within the soil of the said wood or pasture, or in the dyke of the said close, and that the prior and convent might take and impound any cattle in the said close and dyke, and take pledges of any delinquents in the same, except that, if it should happen that the cattle of the said John or his heirs, or cattle agisted in the hay, should enter through default of the enclosure, in such case they should go free and that they might repair the ditches and hays of the close when needful, provided that the deer of the said John and his heirs should have clear exit and entry; saving always to the said John and his heirs the ground (*fundo*) and soil of the said close with the venison of deer found there: the king, therefore, for 5 marks paid by the said prior and convent, has restored to them all the wood and common of pasture of the said close and all the other profits specified above.[2]

[1] *Cal. Pat. Rolls*, 1367–70, p. 68.

[2] *Ibid.* 1367–70, p. 405.

According to this, the monastery had acquired almost every advantage which it could have derived from the actual possession of the land, yet, apparently because this was withheld, the transaction did not amount to an alienation in mortmain. In examining this remarkable grant, one cannot escape the suspicion that it was a deliberate attempt to evade the Statute of Mortmain, but whether or not the suspicion is just, and whatever may have been gained by the arrangement, the fact that it did not pass unnoticed, and that an inquisition was held before the prior and convent were allowed to retain the rights which John Fauconberg had given them, is valuable evidence of the care that was taken to prevent infringements of the statute.

From the examples here cited, it seems clear that the obtaining of a royal licence was a real necessity. Those who made grants to the church without the king's assent might for a time escape notice, but, sooner or later, some vigilant escheator would be sure to hear of the transaction and take possession of the property in the king's name. To recover it would then require more trouble and expense than would have been needed to obtain the neglected licence. But the grantor who sought to provide for his soul's welfare without having regard to the law of mortmain ran a further risk. If his alienation was discovered only after he was dead, and when there was no one powerful enough or interested enough to procure the necessary pardon, the pious gift might be bestowed on some courtier, or go to enrich some ecclesiastics in the king's favour. Then the works of piety, for which the original grant had provided, might remain undone, and his soul would for ever lose those benefits which the gift had been intended to procure. When the pardons and forfeitures are compared with the ordinary licences, it is seen that very few persons cared to run such risks, and that the vast majority of alienations in mortmain were made with the king's assent.

Thus it appears that though the Statute of Mortmain did not prevent, or perhaps even lessen, the acquisitions of land by the church, it succeeded in securing to the crown some control over the grants and an opportunity of obtaining some profit from them.

The facts we have just observed with regard to the enforcement of this statute may be taken as an illustration of the working of many other statutes of this period. It has been said that "all medieval laws were rather enunciations of an ideal than measures which practical statesmen aimed at carrying out in detail".[1] In a sense this is true, for large numbers of persons disobeyed many statutes with impunity, but the failure to enforce the laws was not the result of negligent or inefficient administration as those terms are commonly understood. It may be regarded rather as another aspect of the medieval custom of granting liberties to special persons. Laws, when they were issued, were intended to be enforced, and the administrative machinery for ensuring their observance was fairly adequate, but from time to time it was found more profitable or otherwise desirable to sell or give away an exemption than to enforce the law. If the officers of the crown were as vigilant in detecting and bringing to justice those who had violated other statutes without licence, as they appear to have been in the case of those who had infringed the Statute of Mortmain, the laws must have been enforced with creditable strictness. The grant or sale of numerous exemptions naturally appears to the modern student, accustomed to a state in which the law is the same for all men, flagrant violations of the law. But, imperfect as a system which allowed such exceptions must have been, a state in which it was necessary to procure a formal grant of exemption represents a great advance beyond mere lawlessness.

From what has been said above, it seems clear that few alienations in mortmain can have been made without the king's assent, and it follows that the licences which the Patent Rolls contain may be taken as a fairly reliable guide to the amount of property that was passing into the church's possession, and they also throw a good deal of light on the purposes for which the property was acquired.

One of the first points to be determined is whether, as has often been supposed, an alienation in mortmain always represented a gift to the church. In this connection, it is important to observe that many of the alienations recorded did not increase the property of the church as a whole, but were merely transfers of land or rent from one ecclesiastical corporation to another. That licences should be required for such transactions is, at first,

[1] T. F. Tout, *The Political History of England*, 1216–1377, p. 152.

surprising, for the statute was originally concerned with fresh acquisitions by the church and not with the question of which ecclesiastical body should hold land and rent that was already in mortmain. But if one religious house granted some of its property to another, the amount due to the king when the temporalities should be taken into his hands might be altered and, moreover, the king's control over the church's acquisition of fresh property was probably the more easily maintained if all ecclesiastical corporations were obliged to seek his assent before any changes in the amount of their land or rent could be made. Whether these or other motives led to the requirement, according to the interpretation of the statute by which fourteenth-century administrators were guided, the king's licence seems to have been as necessary for transfers of property already in mortmain as it was for entirely new alienations of land and rent.

The reasons leading ecclesiastical corporations to make grants of this kind to one another were various. A number of religious houses alienated small annual pensions to bishops, most frequently to the bishops of Lincoln, in compensation for the losses which the latter would sustain by the appropriation of churches in their diocese, and sometimes for unspecified benefits which the bishops had conferred on their houses.[1] Not infrequently, also, these alienations were exchanges of property of approximately equal value,[2] but there were many alienations the motives for which are less apparent. For example, in 1344, a licence was issued to enable the prior and convent of Coventry to grant in mortmain to the Carmelite friars of Coventry a toft in that town for the enlargement of their dwelling.[3] Nothing is said about compensation to the prior and convent for the loss of their toft, but in view of the usual rivalry between the various religious orders, it seems quite likely that the monks of Coventry would not have sacrificed any of their possessions to benefit a house of friars without receiving something in return. One is thus led to suspect that the toft may in reality have been purchased.

When the alienations of property which were not at the time held in mortmain are examined, it appears that they were often

[1] See, for example, *Cal. Pat. Rolls*, 1343–45, p. 443; 1345–48, p. 54.
[2] *Ibid.* 1327–30, p. 544; 1338–40, p. 470. [3] *Ibid.* 1343–45, p. 209.

made for reasons similar to those we have discussed above. Thus several of the king's grants in mortmain were in compensation for tithes which had formerly been received from land which he intended to impark. Again, a parcel of land was often granted in mortmain in exchange for property of the same value the grantees already held elsewhere, and in one instance a grant was made to the abbot and monks of Croyland for their licence to alienate certain land which was held of them to a hospital.[1]

Occasionally, the licences state definitely that land or rent had been purchased in mortmain. The grant to Richard Alban, already cited, affords one example of a purchase in mortmain, and, as another, the following item from the Patent Rolls of 1375 may be quoted.

> Pardon to the prior and convent of the friars of the house of the order of preachers of Truro, co. Cornwall, of the foundation of the king's ancestors of the forfeiture incurred by them in purchasing in mortmain from Richard Cristofre two plots of land, not held in chief, containing 100 feet in length and fifty feet in breadth, entering therein and enclosing the same for the enlargement of the close of their manse.[2]

Moreover, purchases may have been made far more frequently than the records imply, as they were primarily concerned with the fact that property was passing into mortmain, and not with the arrangements that were leading to this change. Editors of cartularies have often shown that lands acquired by the Religious in this period and earlier were, in fact, purchased; and there is evidence of money payments, even for grants that were made with the avowed object of benefiting the grantor's soul.[3]

I believe indeed that except in the case of grants to religious houses by their founders or patrons, a purchase may be suspected whenever the purpose of the alienation in mortmain was not specified, or when the purpose was not the provision of any usual work of piety. This view may seem to imply an ungenerous estimate of medieval character. Doubtless there were persons at the time whose zeal for the welfare of the church or of particular ecclesiastics would lead them to confer gifts without

[1] *Cal. Pat. Rolls*, 1358–61, p. 93. [2] *Ibid.* 1374–77, p. 163.

[3] On this point see the conclusions of M. Jacques Laurent in his edition of the Molesme Cartularies, *Cartulaires de l'Abbaye de Molesme*, I, pp. 41, 42.

requiring the performance of any services in return. But medieval men believed so firmly in the efficacy of masses, alms and other conventional good works, done in the interests of their own and other persons' souls, that the altruistic were far more likely to establish such pious works for the souls of their friends and benefactors than to bestow their property unconditionally on any ecclesiastical foundation. At any rate, it is clear from the facts cited above that some at least of the alienations in mortmain represent purchases by the ecclesiastics who received them, and not gifts prompted by devotion.

As might have been expected, a very large proportion of the licences for alienations in mortmain were issued in favour of monks, nuns and regular canons. The property which they were thus allowed to acquire was said to be for a number of different objects and came into their hands in a variety of ways. When the licences which permitted exchanges of property and grants in compensation for tithes, and which probably did not increase the wealth of the church, are left out of account, we find that the licences for grants in mortmain and the pardons for having acquired property in mortmain without licence, which the possessionist orders received, numbered about 1150. Of these more than 300 were for the support of some specified work of piety for the soul of the grantor or of others. Most of such grants were to maintain chantries or have anniversaries celebrated; sixty-two were to maintain lamps or "torches", *i.e.* wax tapers, and in some twenty cases a monastery was made the trustee of a sum to be spent in alms to the poor. The property from whose revenues such good works were to be supported was almost certainly given to the Religious, and there is reason to believe that in many cases its value was considerably in excess of the amount which they were required to expend, so that some profit would accrue to the grantees. The evidence on this point which concerns monastic chantries will be discussed in the next chapter; and here it may be observed that the amount of land or rent alienated to maintain a wax light sometimes seems to have been almost sufficient to pay the wages of a chaplain. Thus the monks who became responsible for these pious works were often considerably enriched thereby.

Some persons were careful to lay down precisely how they

wished the surplus to be spent. Thus in 1370, Denise de Ty obtained a licence to grant certain land and rent to the prioress and nuns of Campsey to celebrate on the fifth of October, her anniversary and those of four other persons, mentioned by name, "the prioress distributing the profits of the premises, beyond the necessary costs of the said anniversaries, among the nuns equally for their habit and clothes".[1] But as a rule the convent which had undertaken such a duty was left free to dispose of the surplus revenue as it thought fit.

Nearly two-thirds of the mortmain licences that concern the monasteries sanctioned grants which appear to have imposed no specific obligations on the recipients. Sometimes the records suggest that the grantor, while requiring no precise service in return for his gift, expected to be remembered in the convent's prayers. In 1363, for example, Edward III granted in mortmain to the prior and convent of Hinton "that they be the more strongly bound to pray for the good estate of the king, Queen Philippa and the king's children, for their souls when they shall have departed this life and the souls of the king's progenitors, kings of England,...a tun of wine yearly in the port of Bristol".[2] A few alienators, who seem to have required nothing of the grantees, gave the property to meet some particular item of monastic expense, and though these grants cannot be proved to have been charitable gifts the language of the licences leads us to believe that they were so. Such was the licence issued in 1360

> out of compassion for the state of the prioress and nuns of the priory of Sywardesleye whose goods and possessions are in these days insufficient for their sustenance, for the alienation in mortmain to them by John Vynter, 'chivaler', of two shops and 6*s*. 4*d*. of rent in Norhampton, of 2*s*. 8*d*. of rent there out of a messuage...and 13*s*. 4*d*. of rent out of a shop...and of the reversions of the said messuages and shop, to hold in aid of their vesture.[3]

Here we may note also that occasionally, though rarely, a convent would receive a pension on behalf of one of its members. Grants by the king of such pensions to monasteries in which political prisoners or members of the royal family were professed are well known, and there is evidence that some other persons

[1] *Cal. Pat. Rolls*, 1370–74, p. 6.
[2] *Ibid.* 1361–64, p. 409.
[3] *Ibid.* 1358–61, p. 436.

made like grants for the benefit of their kinsfolk. One of these cases we learn of through a royal

> Inspeximus and confirmation of letters patent of Edward le Despenser,...dated 20 March, 41 Edward III, granting in mortmain to the abbot of Glastyngbury a rent of 100*s*. out of his manor of Sherston, co. Wilts. for the life of his uncle, William la Zouche, fellow monk of the abbot, for the profit of the latter.[1]

One grant in mortmain in the year 1376, unimportant in itself, is of interest as a reflection of the work of the Good Parliament; this was an "Assignment in mortmain to the abbot and monks of St Mary Graces by the Tower of London, of the tenements and gardens which Richard Lyons had on Le Tourhull by the abbey and which have come into the king's hand for certain causes".[2]

By far the largest number of licences, however, simply allow grants in mortmain to the monasteries, and mention neither services to be done in return, nor how the Religious proposed to use the additional revenue. No doubt the monks owed some of these acquisitions to the charity of the faithful, but, as has been indicated above, there is reason to believe that they secured many of the grants by purchase. It is, however, quite impossible to form any estimate of the proportion of purchases to genuine gifts, and it follows that the mortmain licences are less satisfactory evidence than has sometimes been supposed, as to the esteem in which the Religious were held. Something as to the degree of confidence felt in the religious orders may be inferred from the extent to which they were entrusted with the maintenance of specified works of piety and from the founding of new houses, but the numerous grants of which the purpose is not stated should be left out of account.

In the years that followed the Black Death, the number of licences sanctioning alienations to the monasteries, both for the support of works of piety and for no specified object, tended to decrease. But there was no sudden falling off, and the diminution was not proportionately greater than the diminution of grants for other ecclesiastical purposes, or than one might expect to find in a country impoverished by repeated visitations of pestilence, and the heavy taxes which the war with France necessitated.

[1] *Cal. Pat. Rolls*, 1374–77, p. 438. [2] *Ibid.* 1374–77, p. 343.

Mortmain licences on behalf of the four mendicant orders also frequently appear on the Patent Rolls. Many of the grants which they sanctioned might have been approved even by persons who wished the friars to remain poor. The Dominicans of Shrewsbury and Chelmsford, the Carmelites of Gloucester and Cambridge, and the Augustinians of Bristol, each obtained a licence to receive in mortmain a well, and to make a conduit to their house.[1] Most commonly the licence was sought in order that some convent might enlarge its dwelling-place, and often the property which they were thus allowed to acquire consisted only of a messuage or a small plot of land adjacent to their house, such as might be really necessary to a growing community. Other licences, however, were less in accordance with the friars' profession of poverty, and suggest that some houses aimed at possessing spacious grounds, or perhaps at having a few acres of their own under cultivation. Thus the Carmelites of Snitterley obtained four licences for alienations in mortmain for the enlargement of their manse,[2] and if all these took effect, the convent must have acquired about sixteen acres of land. This house seems to have acquired a larger area than any other during our period, but licences for the grant in mortmain of ten or twelve acres were issued in favour of several other houses.

Fifteen of the licences allowed grants of land on which new friaries were to be built, and in every case but one it is stated or implied that the order had not previously possessed a house in the place. By these licences, if they were fulfilled, the Franciscans were established at Ware (1338); the Augustinians at Droitwich (1331), Clifton Dartmouth (1331), Northallerton (1340), Sherborne (1343), Stafford (1344), Barnstaple (1353) and Rye (1363); the Carmelites at Taunton (1341), Coventry (1342), Ludlow (1350), Doncaster (1350), Drayton in Hales (1354) and Northallerton (1356); and the Dominicans at Worcester (1346).[3] Friars of the last-named order also obtained a licence for the building of a new house in 1339, but under different circumstances. The licence sanctioned an alienation in franc-almoin to

[1] *Cal. Pat. Rolls*, 1364–67, p. 159; 1340–43, pp. 227, 255; 1350–54, pp. 18, 350.

[2] *Ibid.* 1327–30, p. 453; 1330–34, p. 156; 1334–38, p. 405; 1350–54, p. 322.

[3] The dates given in parentheses are the dates of the licences.

the prior and friars preachers of Winchelsea of six acres of land to dwell in and erect houses, oratories and other buildings, and in conclusion stated that "This licence is granted because their dwelling-place is now situated in a place far distant from the town, for which reason the men of the town and others coming to it rarely come to that dwelling-place to hear service and the alms contributed by them are smaller for this cause".[1]

We may be sure that the land on which these new friaries were to be built was given by pious founders for whose souls the convent would promise to pray, but in only one instance is a definite obligation to pray for the givers of such land expressed in the licence. This was a licence of 1363 by which Benedict Zely, Henry Zely and William Taillour were permitted to grant in mortmain to the prior provincial and Austin friars in England two acres of land whereon there used to be five messuages held in chief, which messuages are now destroyed by the sea and worth nothing, "to build thereon an oratory and manse for friars of the Order to augment the divine cult and to celebrate divine service for the good estate of the king and the said Benedict, Henry and William, and for their souls, when they are departed this life, and for the souls of their progenitors and heirs".[2] In fact, judging from the mortmain licences, the friars seem seldom to have received permanent endowments for the maintenance of conventional works of piety such as were constantly undertaken by the other religious orders and by the secular clergy. In 1328, a licence was obtained to grant a messuage in Marlborough to the Carmelite friars there, for the maintenance of a light.[3] By a licence of 1349, Thomas de Fencotes was enabled to grant to the Carmelite friars of London a messuage with appurtenances adjoining their dwelling-place, "for the enlargement of the said dwelling-place and the new work or fabric of their church now begun there in honour of the Virgin Mary, and for a perpetual celebration of divine service for his good estate, for his soul when he is departed from this world and for the soul of Joan late his wife".[4] In the following year, Hugh de Courtenay, the earl of Devon, obtained licence to grant a plot of land to the same convent "to enlarge their dwelling-place

[1] *Cal. Pat. Rolls*, 1338–40, p. 239.
[2] *Ibid.* 1361–64, p. 440.
[3] *Ibid.* 1327–30, p. 333.
[4] *Ibid.* 1348–50, p. 420.

and for a celebration of the anniversary of the earl's son Hugh for ever".[1] In 1373, the king granted to the Augustinian friars of Huntingdon a cart-load of underwood, weekly, because they had "undertaken to have celebrated daily in their own church within their house at the altar of St Augustine a mass of the Trinity for the weal of the king and his sons, and for their souls when they are dead, and for the souls of the late queen Philippa and the king's progenitors".[2] In 1376, the Austin friars of Cambridge secured the restoration of a messuage and a toft, which were forfeit to the crown because they had acquired them in mortmain without licence, on condition that they and their successors celebrated anniversaries of the king, after his death, and of his late consort.[3] With these exceptions, six in number, all the property which the friars received with the royal assent during our period seems to have been acquired without incurring any definite obligations towards the grantors. It is surprising to find so few arrangements of this kind recorded on the Patent Rolls. The friars may, of course, have promised to their benefactors spiritual advantages which the records do not mention, but however this may have been, the freedom from recorded obligations of most of their acquisitions appears in marked contrast to the conditions under which the other religious orders were in the habit of acquiring property, since the latter pledged themselves to the support of some pious work in approximately one out of every four licences which they received.

Another striking difference between the acquisitions of the friars and of the older religious orders has already been suggested, and doubtless arose from the difference in their rules. The monks and canons lived largely from the profits of their estates, and consequently a gift of land or rent in any part of the country was acceptable; while convents of the mendicant orders, though the size of their holdings would have shocked St Francis or St Dominic, were still so far true to their profession that they rarely acquired property which could not be incorporated in their manses. Only two of the licences issued during Edward III's reign may fairly be regarded as indicating departures from this custom. One of these, issued in 1336, confirmed an alienation

[1] *Cal. Pat. Rolls*, 1348–50, p. 512. [2] *Ibid.* 1370–74, p. 236.
[3] *Ibid.* 1374–77, p. 393.

to the Dominicans of Oxford of mills and land;[1] the other, which occurred some four years later, allowed the Carmelite friars of Holne by Alnwick to receive twenty shillings of rent there.[2] But according to the mortmain licences, these were the only cases in which friars were acquiring property as a source of revenue. In this fact we may find an explanation of the rarity of specific obligations, laid down in the mortmain licences. There is plenty of evidence to prove that the friars had many benefactors, and that their prayers were much desired,[3] but the gifts which they received were probably most frequently in money or in goods, out of which alms the friars may well have purchased for themselves much of the land they required. It is, of course, certain that some of the friars' acquisitions of land were genuine gifts, and one interesting mortmain licence shows that persons desiring to assist a house of friars in this way might take considerable trouble to secure for them property which they could hold with advantage. This is a

Licence for the alienation in mortmain by William de Brickhull, citizen of Chester, and Ciceley his wife to the prioress and nuns of Chester of (1) a plot of land 82 feet long by 72 feet broad, in exchange for a plot 102 feet long by 32 feet broad, adjoining the dwelling-house of the Friars Minors of Chester, and (2) of the latter plot to the guardian and Friars Minors for the enlargement of their said dwelling-house.[4]

Whether many other persons acquired land adjoining that of a house of friars for the purpose of conferring it on the convent there is nothing to indicate, but in many grants there are circumstances which suggest purchases rather than gifts. Several licences which they obtained were for grants from other ecclesiastical bodies who, both on account of the hostility which usually existed between the different orders, and because the head of a religious house was bound by oath not to dissipate the goods of his monastery, would be unlikely to give land to the friars without receiving adequate compensation. The pardon to the Dominicans of Truro already cited, moreover, gives us one definite example of a purchase from a layman. Some licences

[1] *Cal. Pat. Rolls*, 1334–38, p. 236. [2] *Ibid.* 1340–43, p. 21.
[3] A. G. Little, *Studies in English Franciscan History*, p. 84.
[4] *Cal. Pat. Rolls*, 1330–34, p. 360.

also show traces of a definite plan of enlarging the premises, which, when once it had been formed, was slowly carried out as opportunities occurred. The clearest example of this is a licence of 1376 for a grant to the Carmelites of Ipswich in full satisfaction of a licence of the late king for them to acquire twelve plots lying around their house for its enlargement.[1]

Forfeitures of property which the friars had acquired without licence, and pardons for the same offence, are to be found on the Patent Rolls, and in two cases the details, which have been recorded, show the friars in a less favourable light than any other ecclesiastics appear in similar records. From time to time members of the secular clergy and of all the religious orders trespassed against the crown in acquiring land or rent without licence, but a more deliberate fraud is suggested in the case of the Carmelite friars of Ludlow who, after the king had granted a licence for the alienation in mortmain to them of one messuage, "by colour of such licence had entered into seven other messuages adjoining such messuage without having obtained his licence for this". These friars were pardoned and allowed to retain the messuages "that they may pray for the good estate of him [the king], his consort and children and for their souls when they are dead",[2] but in the other case, where intentional dishonesty may be suspected, the offenders, the Austin friars of Winchester, were less fortunate. The story of their misdeed is best told in a portion of a writ addressed to the escheator in the county of Southampton directing him to hold an inquisition concerning their acquisitions:

the friars for more than two hundred years, it is said, held a suitable house in the suburb of Winchester, well built and contiguous to the city, in which many bodies of nobles and others lie buried, and certain nobles and others granted many goods for celebrating divine service there for their souls; and by false suggestion the brethren obtained from the king a charter of licence to acquire certain plots in that city, 80 perches in length and 60 perches in breadth, to build a dwelling for themselves there, the king not being informed of whom those plots are held or of the damage which he and others might incur thereby, or that they had another dwelling in that suburb; and now the king has learned that those plots are held of him in chief by a ferm and are charged to others in certain yearly rents, that they are well

[1] *Cal. Pat. Rolls*, 1374–77, p. 385. [2] *Ibid.* 1354–58, p. 299.

built in the better part of the city, adjoining the highway there, that they contain a great part of the city, and that the friars, abandoning their first dwelling by reason of the said licence, have demolished the houses built upon those plots from which the king's ferm and the rents of others used to arise from the inhabitants, whereof a great part of the tallage of the city and other charges used to be raised, have caused those plots to be enclosed and have begun to erect new houses there for themselves, and if this is suffered the king, the city and others will suffer grave prejudice.[1]

The truth of the accusation that they had obtained the licence "by false suggestion" is substantiated by the original licence, which speaks of the Austin friars as "intending to dwell in Winchester",[2] a phrase which in other cases was used when a new house was to be founded where one did not already exist. At the inquisition it was found that the friars had acquired six tenements with plots, full details as to the rents and tallages due from each being given. It was further stated that

the friars had a suitable house in the suburb of that city for their habitation and they voluntarily departed therefrom, and that the house has deteriorated by their departure and it is 20 perches distant from the said city; and that the friars took many goods to the value of 100*l*. and more, for celebrating divine service for the souls of the departed buried in that house.[3]

As a consequence of what was disclosed at this inquisition, the tenements and plots were seized into the king's hand, and the escheator was ordered

to cause the provincial prior of the said order in England and the prior and convent of the order in the said city to be before the king in chancery...to show cause why the said tenements and plots ought not to remain forfeit by reason of the said trespass and deceit, ...on which day the said priors and convent, being summoned, the said provincial prior and the convent did not come, and brother John de Flore, prior of the friars, appeared in chancery and said nothing why the said tenements and plots should not remain forfeit to the king, wherefore it is considered that they shall remain forfeit for ever.[4]

[1] *Cal. Close Rolls*, 1349–54, p. 484.
[2] *Cal. Pat. Rolls*, 1340–43, p. 200.
[3] *Cal. Close Rolls*, 1349–54, p. 485.
[4] *Ibid*. p. 486.

This property was shortly afterwards granted to the city of Winchester

In consideration of the waste and depression in the city of Winchester from the time when the deadly pestilence last prevailed and of the fact that the citizens who hold the city of the king at farm will not be able to pay the farm without grievous oppression of them and the people of the same city.[1]

The licences, and pardons for having acquired in mortmain without licence, which were issued on behalf of the friars during Edward III's reign, number 173. Of these, twenty-eight were for the Franciscans, thirty-one for the Dominicans, fifty-four for the Carmelites, and sixty for the Augustinians. When the licences are examined year by year, we find that the highest numbers were issued during and immediately after the first appearance of the Black Death; there being eight in 1349, seventeen in 1350, six in 1351, and nine in 1352. In no other years of the reign can we discover more than eight licences or pardons, and that number was reached on only two occasions, 1337 and 1338. The friars are, in fact, the only class of ecclesiastics whose acquisitions seem definitely to have increased at the time of the pestilence. It should be observed that the exceptionally high number reached in 1350 was mainly due to the Carmelites, who obtained thirteen out of the seventeen licences issued. Of these, two were for new foundations, at Ludlow and at Doncaster, two were merely for exchanges of property, and two were for grants made in return for a promise of masses. The mendicant orders, especially the Carmelites, may have been particularly popular, or their many acquisitions may mean that a number of convents, desiring to enlarge their manses, took advantage of this time of economic depression when the value of land may have been temporarily reduced. Most likely both causes helped to account for the high numbers that we see. However this may have been, the period of numerous licences was short, not more than four being issued in any year after 1352.

The differences in the numbers of licences in favour of the various orders may indicate that some were more popular than others, or simply that the Franciscans and Dominicans endeavoured to adhere more strictly to their rule of poverty.

[1] *Cal. Pat. Rolls*, 1350–54, p. 223.

On the whole, the impression left, after one has examined all the licences and pardons that concern the friars, is that their possessions in land were extremely modest when compared with those of even the most poorly endowed houses of the possessionist orders. If the friars were rich, they must have become so through direct gifts in money or in kind, yet, even in their acquisitions of land, we see that the friars had considerably relaxed the rule of poverty under which their predecessors of the early thirteenth century had lived.

A number of licences similar to those just discussed were issued on behalf of the holders of parochial livings. Rather more than half of these licences were for the enlargement of rectories and vicarages, and the remainder to provide habitations for the incumbents in places where previously no fixed dwelling-place had been assigned to them. There is, as a rule, very little evidence as to the circumstances in which these alienations were made, but something may be conjectured from what we know of the parishes and of the men who were incumbents at the time. It is noteworthy that in several cases the licences permitting grants for the enlargement of rectories were issued in favour of important and prosperous clerics, who were better known for their services in the chancery than for their performance of ecclesiastical duties. In 1329, for example, we find a licence for the alienation in mortmain to Thomas de Sibthorp, rector of Beckingham, of a toft and two and a half acres of land contiguous to the rectory, for its enlargement.[1] Sibthorp at this time was prominent among the king's clerks.[2] He was engaged in founding a chantry of such dimensions that it became in fact a collegiate church, and some of the ordinances laid down for its government show him to have been a man of more than ordinary generosity, for they include a provision for a distribution of bread to the poor of the parish on three days in each week and, an almost unique requirement, that one of the chaplains should celebrate daily for the souls of the parishioners.[3] It seems quite natural that such a man should endeavour to improve the benefice which he held, and the grant of land which the licence

[1] *Cal. Pat. Rolls*, 1327–30, p. 387.
[2] B. Wilkinson, *The Chancery under Edward III*, pp. 162, 163.
[3] *V.C.H. Nottingham*, II, pp. 150–2.

sanctioned was most likely obtained as a purchase by Sibthorp himself. We know less about the other rectors whose manses were being enlarged, but a number of them were royal clerks of some importance. To add to the value or convenience of benefices held by men of this type to whom the parish was often little more than a source of revenue, could hardly be regarded as a work of piety, inspired by devotion to the church, and the most likely explanation of the grants that occur is that they represent improvements which the rectors themselves were making.

The need of large manses for parsons who were unlikely to reside may not at first be apparent. But the rector, besides requiring a house in which he could dwell if he chose, and where, on occasion, guests might be entertained, would need to possess a safe place wherein to store his tithes, which, of course, were largely paid in kind. To meet this necessity, the rector of a large parish would sometimes acquire land in some outlying part of it. We read of one such acquisition in a licence of 1356, sanctioning an alienation in mortmain to Master William de Excestre, parson of the church of Croston, of an acre of land in the town of Chorley, which is in the parish of the said church, to build houses to store the tithes of Chorley and other neighbouring towns of the parish, which are far distant from the rectory of the said church.[1]

This need of buildings in which the tithes might be kept safely, probably accounts for the fact that in many cases when a church was served by a vicar, he dwelt, not in the house of the absent rector, but in another that had been specially assigned to him. During our period some twenty licences occur which allowed grants in mortmain with the object of giving a settled dwelling-place to vicars. In five of these, the language suggests that the vicar's house was actually to be built; in the other cases, it seems more likely that the vicars were receiving land on which buildings had already been erected. Several of the alienators, both ecclesiastical bodies and individual persons, were the rectors of the parishes concerned, and the grants which they made were probably in fulfilment of agreements with regard to their vicars' stipends. In some cases, notably that of Cranbrook,[2] the church

[1] *Cal. Pat. Rolls*, 1354–58, p. 344. [2] *Ibid.* 1361–64, p. 52.

whose vicar was thus provided for had been comparatively recently appropriated,[1] but it is surprising to find that one of the vicars to whom a habitation was assigned was Henry Bentbowe, vicar of St Mary's, Scarborough,[2] which the abbot and convent of Cîteaux, the appropriators, held by a grant of Richard I in aid of the expenses of their general chapters.[3]

Some parishes also seem to have lacked manses for their rectors. A mortmain licence for a grant to the rector of Elmswell contains the phrase "to which church there has hitherto been no certain domicile annexed for the stay of the rectors there",[4] and similar language is used in a grant to the rector of St Thomas's, Winchelsea.[5] Two other licences permitted grants of land on which houses for the rectors were to be built, and in thirteen others, such phrases as "for his habitation" occur and imply that until that time the parsons had not possessed dwelling-places.

The ground for enlarging the manses of some of the parochial clergy was given in return for services which the priests were to render. Thus a licence of 1340 sanctioned a grant to John de Scotenay, vicar of the church of St Mary, Crakepool, of a plot of land 60 feet square for the enlargement of his dwelling-place, "that he may celebrate divine service in the said church for the souls of the said Ranulph [de Burton] and Alice his wife [the alienators of the land] on their anniversary day".[6]

We meet also with alienations to rectors and vicars of property which was probably intended to increase the value of the benefice rather than to add to the convenience of the manse. One licence in which this is definitely expressed occurs in 1355. By it, the king assented to an alienation in mortmain to Nicholas, vicar of the church of Wichingham St Mary, of a plot of land 156 feet long by 86 feet wide, for the enlargement of the manse of his vicarage and of an acre and a half of land and a rood and a half of meadow, "in aid of his sustenance for ever".[7] Since the fine of ten shillings, exacted for this licence, was paid by Nicholas, one suspects that the grant may have represented a purchase

1 *Cal. Papal Letters*, II, p. 198.
2 *Cal. Pat. Rolls*, 1361–64, p. 241.
3 *Memorials of Fountains Abbey*, II, p. 11 n.
4 *Cal. Pat. Rolls*, 1350–54, p. 111.
5 *Ibid.* 1348–50, p. 369.
6 *Ibid.* 1338–40, p. 478.
7 *Ibid.* 1354–58, p. 266.

which he had made, but there is nothing to prove that this was so, and it may be hoped that in at least some of the licences of this kind we see the charitable work of men who, like the good knight commemorated by Gascoigne, were bestowing land and tenements on poorly endowed parishes in order that their priests should be adequately maintained.[1]

A considerable number of licences allowed alienations in mortmain to the chapters of secular cathedrals and of collegiate churches. But to discuss these licences in detail would be unprofitable, since they add little to what is already known. The purposes for which land or rent was granted to them did not differ from those for which the monks received endowments, except that the chapters of Crediton and most of the secular cathedrals obtained one or more licences for grants in support of the vicars choral. It is noteworthy, too, that in few cases were the grants made to these corporations of seculars, free from conditions.

Licences were also frequently issued for the endowment of hospitals, especially at the beginning of our period; and some of these grants were, no doubt, among the most charitable deeds of which we have record. A few licences expressly state that the grant is to benefit the poor or the sick in the hospital, but more frequently the purpose was said to be the endowment of a chantry in the chapel of the hospital. Many licences also contain no information as to how the property was to be used, and while, in some cases, the grants which they allowed doubtless assisted the poor, it is to be feared that in others they merely enriched the master, or added to the comforts of the priests serving under him.

In our discussion of the alienations in mortmain to the various classes of ecclesiastics, something has naturally been said with regard to the interests and motives of the grantors, and here it may be well to summarize briefly what the mortmain licences reveal concerning this subject. As has already been observed, the majority of grants of which the purpose has been recorded were in aid of some work of piety which would benefit the soul of the grantor or of those in whom he was interested. The founding and endowing of monasteries, colleges and hospitals must, of

[1] *Loci e Libro Veritatum*, ed. J. E. T. Rogers, p. 149.

course, be reckoned among such good works, but the facts concerning those that were established within our period are already too well known to need repetition here.

Some alienations in mortmain, while procuring spiritual advantages for the grantor, also contributed towards the temporal well-being of the community. This is especially true of the gifts to hospitals, and to the Oxford and Cambridge colleges, and of a number of small grants in support of charities. The maintenance of these charities was usually entrusted to hospitals or monasteries. For example, in 1369, a licence was issued allowing the alienation in mortmain to the prior and convent of Norwich

> by Nicholas Note, chaplain, and Laurence Crank, chaplain, of a messuage, 34 acres of land, 2 acres of pasture, 2 acres of turbary, and 2½ acres of marsh,...of the clear yearly value of 8*s*. to distribute 8*s*. yearly at Great Yarmouth on the eve of St Nicholas the Bishop to 152 poor persons, to wit one half-penny to each (*sic*), for the good estate of the said chaplains and for their souls when they shall have departed this life.[1]

This grant is of peculiar interest, because the two chaplains who made it, appear to have been among the very few persons of that time who were willing that all their benefaction should be spent on the poor, without requiring either the burning of lights or the saying of masses on their own behalf. For in the majority of cases, those who were made responsible for such charities were directed also to provide out of the revenues for such services. Moreover, licences in which alms are mentioned at all occur only rarely. Far more frequently, the alienation in mortmain was intended to procure only spiritual benefits for the grantor and those who were associated with him. The provisions for votive lights occur much oftener than those for distributions to the poor, and most frequently of all, we meet with the endowment of masses. In fact, the strongest impression that one receives from a study of the mortmain licences of this period is of the immense importance attached to the saying of masses. If a hospital was founded, one of the first provisions would be for one or more chaplains who would celebrate for the souls of the benefactors of the house; and the like duties were assigned to

[1] *Cal. Pat. Rolls*, 1367–70, p. 215.

the chaplains of university colleges. The two principal monastic foundations of the time, the houses of Maxstoke and Edingdon, both originated as chantries, and in both the canons may fairly be regarded as established mainly to fulfil the duties of chantry priests. The chantries, however, are so important, and the material concerning them which the mortmain licences contain, so abundant, that it has seemed advisable to make them the subject of a separate chapter.

CHAPTER IV

CHANTRIES

OF all the institutions that grew up in the medieval church, there is probably none concerning which our knowledge is so indefinite as the chantry. Beautiful chapels like those in Winchester Cathedral remain to remind us of the important part played by the chantries in the religious life of the Middle Ages, and many individual chantries have been fully described in the histories of the churches to which they belonged; but the enquirer looks in vain for an English monograph on the subject as a whole, or even for adequate treatment of it in the histories of the English church. Rock, in his *Church of Our Fathers*, does indeed devote several pages to the medieval chantry, but in this part of his work he appears to have consulted no manuscript sources, and at the time when he wrote there was not sufficient material in print for a satisfactory study of this subject. Moreover, his religious enthusiasm led him, unconsciously perhaps, to paint an idealistic picture which, when examined in the light of the fuller evidence now available, is easily seen to be a most unfaithful likeness. Among the more recent writers who have described medieval chantries, the late Canon Westlake is the most instructive, but he was concerned only with those chantries which were maintained by the guilds, and there are, therefore, many aspects of chantry history with which he did not attempt to deal.

The work of these and other writers has, in fact, been just sufficient to convey a general impression of the purposes for which chantries were founded, and to indicate their great increase in numbers towards the end of the Middle Ages; but beyond this, little has been definitely established.

In recent years, however, much has been done to prepare the way for a more thorough investigation of chantry history, by the publication of much of the material on which such a study would necessarily be based. Borough records, episcopal registers, monastic cartularies and the royal chancery enrolments all contain valuable evidence relating to this subject, and moreover, a vast amount of information with regard to the chantries on the eve of their suppression has been collected and preserved in the famous Chantry Certificates. Many of these latter are now available in print, in the transactions of local societies, and fortunately some of the editors have interpreted their task very liberally and have added, in notes and appendices, all that they could discover of the previous history of the chantries which the certificates concerned. But they have left to others the task, as yet unaccomplished, of writing from this material the history of the chantry as an institution.

An adequate account of the chantry system would be far beyond the scope of the present work, but a discussion of the evidence relating to chantries which the official records of our period contain forms a necessary part of this study, and this evidence, though it still leaves much unexplained, is sufficient to provide material for a more detailed account of the English chantries, at least during one half-century of their history, than has so far been given.

Here, as in the preceding chapter, our principal source will be the licences for alienations in mortmain, and it follows that the chantries with which we shall be mainly concerned were those which were established by a permanent endowment of land or rent. This class is far from including all the chantries which were established. There were, in the first place, as will appear from a study of any considerable collection of medieval wills, many foundations which may be called temporary chantries, that is, which were to be kept up during a specified period, often for one year, or for three years, and which were paid for by a bequest of a sum of money, sufficient, in the grantor's opinion, to pay the priest or priests for their services during the appointed time.

Another class of chantries, with which we shall have little to do, were those maintained by the guilds. These were, indeed, intended to be perpetual chantries, and some of them received permanent endowments of land or rent, but more frequently, as Westlake's study of the religious guilds has shown, the chaplain's stipend was paid out of the guild's funds, most of which were derived from the entrance fees and annual subscriptions of its members. With these chantries, also, the mortmain licences are seldom concerned. But when due allowance has been made for all the chantries of this kind which may have been established, it still appears that by far the greater number of perpetual chantries were provided for by one or more grants in mortmain. Concerning these, there is probably more to be learned from the royal letters sanctioning the endowments than from any other single source. It must be remembered, however, that a licence does not prove that a chantry was actually founded, and in many cases one cannot be sure that the transfer of property, for which permission had been obtained, actually took place. On the other hand, since the procuring of a licence to alienate property in mortmain usually entailed considerable expense, it cannot reasonably be doubted that those who obtained such licences for the endowment of chantries did so with the serious intention of providing in this way for the welfare of their souls. It is certain, also, that in the great majority of cases the gifts which the licences allowed were actually made. The licences are, therefore, of some value as an indication of the numbers of chantries that were being endowed during our period, but their chief importance lies in the incidental information as to how the chantry was to be served, who should present to it, and other similar matters which reveal to us the aims of the founders and the difficulties which they encountered or feared.

The simplest form of licence for the endowment of a chantry is that which occurs most frequently. It contains merely the royal assent to a grant in mortmain of certain property to a chaplain to celebrate divine service daily in a specified place for the souls of one or more persons who are mentioned by name. In these cases, nothing is said as to who should present to the chantry, or whether the priest was to be under any special supervision. We should not, however, infer from this that no patron was appointed, for it probably means only that the founder delayed to state his intentions in this matter until the final regulations of his chantry were drawn up. The foundation deeds suggest that, most commonly, the founder retained the patronage for life, and that after his death it passed to those who might be expected to feel the strongest personal interest in the chantry's continuance, the heirs of its founder. An arrangement of this kind had also the advantage of giving to the founder and his heirs a means of providing for some clerical kinsman or dependant. For that reason, the patronage of chantries was much valued in fourteenth and fifteenth century Germany,[1] and, no doubt, it was found to be equally useful in this country, though our records contain very little information on this subject. Of the few items I have discovered, the most curious is the provision in a will of 1359 by which Nicholas Benyngton, Mercer, bequeathed his capital messuage and shop to his son William, on condition that the latter, before reaching the age of twenty-five, should take holy orders and become a chaplain to pray for his soul: and desired that if this condition was not fulfilled the property should be sold for pious uses.[2] The founders of perpetual chantries occasionally expressed the wish that their chaplains should if possible be men of the parish, but I have met with only three instances in which preference is to be given to members of the founder's family. One of these is the deed by which Robert de Askeby established a chantry at the altar of St John the Baptist in the church of Hale in Lincolnshire, and in which he says:

> Further, with the consent of the abbot and convent of Bardeneye, the patrons of the said church, and of the rector, I ordain that some one of my kindred (*parentela*), if anyone suitable be found, or otherwise that some one of the said parish before any other persons whomsoever, be presented to the bishop by me for this turn, and afterwards, whenever a vacancy occurs, by me for my life and, after my death, by my heirs; and the bishop shall be bound to admit and institute him unless he plainly be shewn to be unsuitable and unworthy.[3]

Occasionally the records show exceptional solicitude of a patron for the welfare and comfort of an individual chaplain, which suggests a tie of kindred or personal friendship. Thus a document of 1371, concerning the establishment of a new chantry in the church of St Martin le Grand, after specifying in detail the amounts which the priest was to receive for his stipend, and the provision that had been made for his dwelling, continues,

[1] Emma Katz, *Mittelalterliche Altarpfründen der Diözese Bremen im Gebiet westlich der Elbe*, p. 23; Georg Matthaei, *Die Vikariestiftungen der Lüneburger Stadtkirchen im Mittelalter und im Zeitalter der Reformation*, p. 11.

[2] *Calendar of Wills proved in the Court of Husting, London*, part ii, p. 52.

[3] Associated Architectural Societies' *Reports*, XXXVII, p. 59; see also *Transactions of the Thoroton Society*, XVII, pp. 70, 71.

"Sir John de Ledbury shall hold the said chantry with appurtenances for life, and shall not be compelled to follow the choir at night time against his will".[1]

Some founders, however, perhaps fearing the failure of heirs, preferred to provide for their chantries by entrusting the patronage, and, often, also the sources of income out of which the priest was to be paid, to a corporation or to the holder of some office. For example, when, in 1335, a chantry was established in the church of St Thomas the Martyr, at Bristol, for the soul of Richard de Welles, late burgess of that town, it was laid down that the right of presenting to the chantry, when void, should belong to the mayor of Bristol for the time being.[2] More often the incumbent and churchwardens of the church in which the chantry was to be situated were entrusted with the duty of finding the priest. Thus in 1342, Matilda, late the wife of William de Caxton, obtained a licence to grant in mortmain certain property to Thomas, parson of the church of St Swithin, Candlewick Street, in London, and four parishioners, wardens of the fabric of the said church, from the profits of which they were to provide a chaplain "to celebrate divine service daily in the church for her good estate, for her soul when she is dead, for the soul of the said William, and the souls of all aiders of the said chantry and fabric".[3] The degree of control which the parson and wardens would be able to exercise over the priest when once he had been appointed is, in this case, not stated, but in the documents concerning the foundation of a slightly earlier chantry the rights of the parson who was to present are clearly set forth. This document was a grant of five marks of rent out of certain tenements, for the support of a chaplain to celebrate divine service daily in the church of St Martin Outwich, London, for the souls of the founder and others, and, in the concluding portion, power was conferred on the rector of the said church to distrain for the rent, if it should be in arrear; to remove the chaplain at any time in case of misconduct; and to present to the chantry whenever it should be void.[4]

In many respects such arrangements, especially when some of

[1] *Cal. Pat. Rolls*, 1371–74, p. 85.
[2] *The Little Red Book of Bristol*, I, p. 212.
[3] *Cal. Pat. Rolls*, 1340–43, p. 467.
[4] *Ibid.* 1330–34, p. 230.

the parishioners were associated with the incumbent in the trust, would seem the most satisfactory that could be devised; since to the founder it gave the advantage of placing his chantry under the control of persons who would have ample opportunity of observing the conduct of its priest, while, at the same time, it placed the rector or vicar in the fortunate position of being able to choose the priest who was to celebrate masses at an altar within his church, recite with him the canonical hours, and who would, naturally, be associated with him in the daily life of the parish.

But in spite of their apparent advantages, agreements of this kind were comparatively rare, and the majority of founders, who did not grant the property to the chantry priest himself and leave the presentation to their heirs, provided for their chantries by endowing monasteries or collegiate churches. This system was fairly popular, about a seventh of the chantries founded within our period being made more or less dependent on some ecclesiastical corporation.

In some cases, the corporation seems to have acted merely as a trustee. For instance, in 1332, a licence was granted

> for the alienation in mortmain by John de Framlyngham, clerk, to the prioress and nuns of Caumpesse, of the manor of Carleton by Keleshale, co. Suffolk, and of the advowson of the church of that town, and for the prioress and nuns to grant the manor to a chaplain, for life, on condition that he, with two other chaplains to be found by him, celebrate divine service daily in the said church for the soul of Alice de Hanaud, late countess of the marshal, aunt of the queen, and for the soul of the grantor, after his death. On the death of the said chaplain, the prioress and nuns are to resume possession of the manor and to grant it to another chaplain to hold upon like conditions, according to the appointment to be made by the said John, and so from time to time as each successive chaplain dies.[1]

In some respects, the terms of the grant just cited appear to be unique. It is the only instance I have discovered in which a manor, and not a fixed sum to be paid in money or in kind, was to be the portion of a chaplain serving under a monastery, and the provision for the resumption of the manor by the prioress and convent on the death of each successive chaplain is a condition not met with elsewhere. Provision for chaplains by means of

[1] *Cal. Pat. Rolls*, 1330–34, p. 266.

a fixed rent, payable by a monastery, was a fairly common arrangement. In these cases, the founder usually granted to a monastery or other ecclesiastical corporation an amount of land or rent, of which the annual income somewhat exceeded the amount to be spent on the chantry, and obtained from the grantees in return a promise to pay to one or more chaplains a specified sum of money. A good example of this kind of grant is afforded by a licence of 1364, whereby Henry le Haute obtained permission to charge the manor of Elmsted, co. Kent, with ten marks yearly, for the prior and convent of St Gregory, Canterbury, to find a chaplain to celebrate divine service as he shall ordain, in the church of Waltham, "on condition that the prior and convent pay to the chaplain and his successors 103*s*. 4*d*. yearly for their sustenance, and that they may charge their manor of Nanynton, not held of the king, with distraint by the chaplain for the said sum if ever it shall fall into arrear".[1] This example is particularly interesting because the sum which the priory was to receive, as well as the chaplain's stipend, are given in terms of money. We see from it that the monastery was to retain thirty shillings in rent for seeing that the chantry priest received his salary. Why Henry le Haute chose to provide for his chantry by this somewhat complicated arrangement, instead of by granting the stipend direct to the chaplain, is not clear, but, as the Patent Rolls and other sources record a number of similar agreements, it seems likely that they were thought to offer some additional security for the welfare of the chantries.

It should be observed, however, that a number of the chantries, whose priests were to be paid by monasteries or other ecclesiastical corporations, were situated in churches appropriated to those bodies, and, in such cases, the maintenance of the chantries may well have been committed to them simply by virtue of their position as rectors. Occasionally this reason is suggested in the documents themselves,[2] though this does not explain why the possibly distant monastery was considered a more suitable trustee than the resident vicar. It may be the result of a desire to confer some benefit on the Religious, or it may indicate a belief that the monasteries would be under less temptation to neglect

[1] *Cal. Pat. Rolls*, 1361–64, p. 474.
[2] *E.g.* see *Ibid*. 1334–38, p. 334.

the chantry and appropriate its fruits to their own uses than would be a possibly underpaid vicar. As might have been expected, the chantries which monasteries were to maintain in churches other than their own were generally served by secular priests, but occasionally, regular canons were to be found performing the duties of chantry priests in churches appropriated to their monasteries. Thus in 1348, a licence was issued for an alienation in mortmain to the abbot and convent of Blanchland "to find a canon of the abbey as chaplain to celebrate divine service daily [for certain souls] in the church of St Wilfred, Kirke Herle which is appropriated to the abbey, ...who shall dwell always with the vicar of the church, a canon of the same abbey".[1] There is no indication of how this arrangement came to be made, or of whether the plan originated with the founder of the chantry, or with the monastery, but it must have been greatly to the latter's advantage. For ecclesiastical law required that a regular canon, who was the vicar of a parish church, should have always with him a fellow canon of the same order. If, then, the fellow canon while fulfilling this duty could be employed as a chantry priest, thus causing his monastery to receive the money that would otherwise have been spent on the support of a secular chaplain, the financial advantage is obvious; and it was probably also far more satisfactory to assign to the canon definite duties of his own than to send him out from the monastery merely as the companion of the vicar.

But the majority of the chantries entrusted to monasteries, whether their priests were seculars or regulars, were to be maintained within the precincts of the monasteries themselves. Of these, a number were to be served by secular priests. This fact raises some difficult questions, which have not, so far, been satisfactorily answered. It has been generally assumed that the prayers of the Religious were, if anything, more effective than those of the secular clergy, and, therefore, that to have one's chantry served by monks or canons was most desirable. From this, the natural inference has been, that when a deed provided that secular priests should serve a chantry within an abbey or priory, it was because the monks there had already undertaken to celebrate as many masses as their numbers permitted, no

[1] *Cal. Pat. Rolls*, 1348–50, p. 208.

priest being allowed by canon law to say mass oftener than once a day. But, in 1398, the pope granted to the prior and chapter of Ely an indult to substitute two monks for the two secular chantry priests, whom they were bound to find, to celebrate masses in the chapel of St Mary the Virgin, in their cathedral church, "the endowment, the condition attached to which they promised to observe, being not enough for the maintenance of the said priests".[1] It is interesting to observe that the monastery was bound to maintain the type of priests that had been originally agreed upon, and that a change from seculars to regulars would be to the monks' advantage. Now, as throughout the fourteenth century the numbers of monks and canons in the religious houses tended to diminish, and as there is nothing to indicate that Ely was an exception to this rule, it does not seem likely that the house contained more monks in 1398 than at the time when the chantries were founded. If this is so, it would seem that the founders of these chantries could, if they had wished, have had them served from the first by monks of the priory, but that they deliberately chose secular priests.

Still more important evidence on this point comes from the records relating to the Montacute chantry which was established in the priory of St Frideswide, at Oxford. In 1346, Elizabeth, formerly the wife of William de Monte Acuto, gave to the prior and convent forty-six acres of meadow which was then known as Stockwell Mead, and which under the name of Christ Church Meadows have now for many generations been famous and beloved. In return for this grant, the prior and canons bound themselves to find for ever two secular priests who should celebrate divine service daily in the chapel of St Mary the Virgin, in their convent church, for the soul of William de Monte Acuto, the good estate of Elizabeth while she lived, and for her soul after her death, and the souls of a number of other persons mentioned by name. One of the chaplains was to receive from the convent ten marks a year for his salary and that of his companion, and for the payment of this sum the canons bound their manor of Hiddon in Berkshire.[2] A little more than a month after this grant was made, Elizabeth de Monte Acuto

[1] *Cal. Papal Letters*, v, p. 159.
[2] *Cartulary of St Frideswide's*, II, pp. 3, 4.

issued another charter on behalf of the canons, by which she authorized them to substitute canons of the house for the secular priests, if the profits of Stockwell Mead should prove insufficient for the support of the latter.[1] For some years the chantry was served by the two secular priests; then, about 1363, the convent obtained permission from the official of Lincoln to keep one secular priest instead of two.[2] This arrangement continued until 1380, when John, bishop of Lincoln, decreed on their petition that two canons of the monastery should thenceforth serve the chantry.[3] This may suggest that the chantry could from the first have been served by canons of St Frideswide's, but that the lady Elizabeth preferred to have secular priests, and agreed to the substitution of canons only in case the endowments she had provided should be found inadequate for the fulfilment of her purpose. Moreover, from the subsequent history of the chantry we see that the canons found it profitable to make the authorized change. Here, then, is a case of a chantry established within the precincts and under the care of a monastery, whose inmates apparently had not already undertaken to celebrate the greatest possible number of masses, yet by the express wish of its founder its priests were to be seculars.

It may be argued, indeed, that in these cases the Religious were suppressing other statutory masses. We do not know what masses either the monks of Ely or the canons of St Frideswide's were pledged to celebrate at the time when the chantries under discussion were established. It is possible, therefore, that the founders knew or suspected that if members of these convents were entrusted with the celebration of the services, some statutory masses would be suppressed, or combined with those which they were founding, as often happened in medieval France.[4] But if the founders had serious doubts as to the good faith of the Religious, it is surprising that they chose to make them the trustees for their chantries, instead of arranging for the endowments to be held directly by secular priests.

The way in which the English monks fulfilled their duties with regard to the celebration of statutory masses has not been

[1] *Cartulary of St Frideswide's*, II, pp. 14, 15.
[2] *Ibid.* pp. 15, 16.
[3] *Ibid.* pp. 15, 16.
[4] Auguste Molinier, *Les Obituaires Français au Moyen Âge*, pp. 133 ff.

subjected to the same careful examination as the conduct of their French brethren in this matter. Yet there is sufficient evidence to show that the problem was acute with us also, though generally church conditions were somewhat better in England than in France. At any rate, it seems to have been easier to procure the celebration of masses here than on the continent. For while many French and German founders established chantries for masses on certain days of each week,[1] in England the daily mass was almost always required.

Although, therefore, we cannot prove that at Ely or St Frideswide's statutory masses were being suppressed, neither can we prove that these convents had not undertaken the greatest possible number of masses. The question is thus left obscure; but it is just possible that the establishment in monastic churches of chantries to be served by secular priests does not necessarily mean that the Religious of the houses could not legally have celebrated more masses.

When the Religious were made responsible for chantries of secular priests, it was customary to leave the patronage in their hands. Exceptions to this practice are, however, occasionally to be found. The most interesting one which the records of our period contain comes from an item in the Patent Rolls of 1345, cancelling letters patent by which John de Kyneton had had licence to grant certain property to a chaplain to celebrate divine service daily in the chapel of Holy Trinity, Kyneton, and allowing him instead "to assign the premises to the abbot of Roche and the convent of that place to find a secular chaplain to celebrate service as above...and for them to grant to him and his heirs a corrody from the abbey for the sustenance of the said chaplain and his successors".[2]

Besides exceptions of this kind, we meet with cases in which the foundation provided for more than one priest, and the religious house presented only one chaplain, who would be the principal chaplain or warden of the chantry, allowing him to choose his companions. An example of this has already been given in the letters patent relating to the chantry at Carlton by

[1] Auguste Molinier, *Les Obituaires Français au Moyen Âge*, pp. 313 ff.; Emma Katz, *Mittelalterliche Altarpfründen*, p. 63.
[2] *Cal. Pat. Rolls*, 1343–45, p. 455.

Kelsale, which the nuns of Campsey were to maintain, and a further illustration may be taken from the prior and convent of St Frideswide's ordinance concerning the Montacute chantry. According to this, the presentation of the principal chaplain was to belong to Elizabeth de Monte Acuto during her life and then to the prior and convent, but the choice of the second chaplain, with power to retain or remove him according to his conduct, was committed to the first chaplain "ut inter eum et socium maior concordia et firmior unitas habeatur".[1]

The proportion of chantries in which the Religious were bound to maintain secular priests is, however, comparatively small. It was far more usual to require only that the monastery which had received the founder's property should support one or more chaplains, without stating whether they were to be seculars or regulars.

A large number of founders, also, desired that the masses for their souls should be celebrated by members of the monastic orders. In many cases, it is clear that the new chantry was not intended to increase the number of monks which the house usually contained, but merely to secure the services of one of its ordinary inmates. Whatever the convent received for such a chantry, whether the sum bestowed amounted to the cost of keeping a monk or not, must have been largely gain, and it is not unlikely, therefore, that a monastery, which still contained members who were not pledged to the celebration of masses, would agree that one of its number should perform the duties of a chantry priest in return for a smaller endowment than would have been necessary for the support of a secular priest. An arrangement of this kind may thus have been one of the least expensive ways of establishing a chantry.

A similar practice was from time to time followed in the founding of chantries to be served by the brethren of hospitals, or by priests already attached to cathedral or other collegiate churches. The vicars choral who were bound to reside and to say the canonical hours in the choirs of their churches, but who were ordinarily under no obligation to celebrate masses, would seem particularly suitable persons for such employment, and they were on several occasions the beneficiaries of grants made on

[1] *Cartulary of St Frideswide's*, II, p. 11.

condition that one of them should celebrate a daily mass for the donor's soul. But there was a legal difficulty in the way of such grants, which may be best explained by the following quotation from the Patent Rolls of 1352:

Whereas the king by letters patent, lately granted licence for the alienation in mortmain by Walter son of John Deneys to the vicars of the church of St Cross, Cryditon, of an acre of land in Bradeford Dabernoun, Prestecote and Chirchedon, and the advowson of the church of All Saints, Bradeford, to find a chaplain to celebrate divine service daily in the chapel of the Holy Trinity, Bradeford, as contained in the letters patent; petition has now been made to him on behalf of John, son and heir of the said Walter, praying that, inasmuch as the latter died before the licence had taken effect, and it had been his principal intention, when alive, by this donation to augment in some degree the portions of the said vicars, which are very slender, and because the vicars, not being perpetual, cannot acquire to themselves in common, the king will grant licence for the said John to assign the said land and advowson to the precentor and chapter of the church of St Cross to augment the portions of the said vicars, on condition that one of them, a priest, celebrate divine service daily in the said church for the souls of the said Walter and his wife,

and a number of other persons who are mentioned by name.[1]

This is the only statement I have discovered of the reasons for conferring on the chapter of a collegiate church a grant which was intended to benefit the vicars, but as endowments for the vicars of other churches were given in the same way, it may be inferred that other vicars besides those of Crediton could not acquire in common. This necessity of making the chapter trustees for funds granted to the vicars may have left the administration of them peculiarly open to abuses. At any rate, provisions for chantries to be served by vicars of collegiate churches are comparatively rare.

A more costly, but perhaps also a more secure method of founding a chantry under the supervision of an ecclesiastical corporation, was to endow a religious house for the maintenance of one or more members, beyond the appointed number, who should be bound to celebrate masses and other services for the founder's soul. In most cases, the choice of such additional monks appears to have been left with the heads of the houses in which they were to dwell, but a curious exception to this rule is

[1] *Cal. Pat. Rolls*, 1350–54, pp. 329, 330.

described in letters patent of 1328. In that year, the earl of Oxford, Robert de Vere, obtained a licence to grant his manor of Manbrig to the abbot and convent of Netley, who were to pay for this an annual rent of twenty pounds, and to find two monks, as chaplains, to celebrate divine service daily in their abbey for the souls of the earl, his ancestors and heirs and other persons. At the same time de Vere was granted a further licence "to present two secular clerks to the said abbot for admission as monks, promotion to the priesthood, and appointment to the said chantries, and to fill up vacancies in like manner".[1] The right of nominating a monk or a nun to a religious house was, in itself, an important and useful privilege, but it is probable that the earl's chief motive in making this agreement with Netley was to obtain additional security for the faithful service of his chantry. A still more definite attempt to secure the special loyalty of a monastic chaplain appears in a mortmain licence of 1342, for the establishment of a chantry at Christchurch, Twynham, according to which, the canon who was to serve it was not only to be presented to the prior by the founder and her heirs, but was to receive annually "13*s*. 4*d*. beyond what the other canons of the priory received".[2]

Such provisions suggest, perhaps, that the founders were not free from fear lest their chantries would be neglected and the funds misapplied, and there are other records which express anxiety on this point in the strongest terms.

Some persons hoped to provide additional security for the maintenance of their chantries by subjecting the priests to exceptionally strict supervision. For instance, John de Harrington, a canon of Lincoln who in 1334 established a chantry in the church of Harrington, under the patronage of his cathedral chapter, required that

> the chaplain and his fellow shall be visited once every year by the chief provost of the chapter of the church of Lincoln in his summer tourn;... And the provost [shall enquire] concerning the life and conversation of both the chaplains, and concerning the adequacy of the stock, and whether they serve as by this ordination they are bound to do for the souls aforesaid, and also concerning the state of the houses, close, oratory, and ornaments aforesaid, and moreover of the land of the

[1] *Cal. Pat. Rolls*, 1327–30, p. 262. [2] *Ibid.* 1340–43, p. 387.

chantry and its other appurtenances,...And if he find any default, he shall take, punish, and correct the chaplains without delay, as far as he can.[1]

In some cases at least, similar rights of supervision were entrusted to the borough officials who held the patronage of chantries. Thus, during our period, several citizens of London bequeathed small annual pensions to the mayor, the recorder, or alderman of a specified ward in return for seeing that the ordinances concerning their chantries were faithfully observed. To what extent similar practices may have been followed in other towns I have not been able to discover, but the records of at least one town, that of Bristol, contain some interesting evidence of the mayor's position with regard to the chantries of his patronage. For in Ricart's Calendar, in which are set forth the customary duties of the mayor, we read:

it hath be vsed, on the iiijth daie aftir Mighelmas, the seide newe Maire to let sommen all the chauntry preestis whos composicions are enrolled in the rede boke; ...to com before the Maire to the Counter, there to take their othes, truly to obserue their seide composicions; and theire seide othes to be made vnder this forme, that is to seie, euery of them to ley his lyfte hand on the boke, and his righte hande on his breste, makyng his othe per sancta euangelia and per verba sacerdotis.[2]

The same work also mentions the obits which the mayor was accustomed to attend, and gives us besides a brief account of the mayor's duties in supervising the affairs of one of the chantries in the town, which were probably very similar to what was done with regard to other chantries in Bristol and elsewhere.

Item, the morowe vpon All Sowlen day, the Maire is vsid to walk to Redclyff, and the Toune clerk with him; there to sytte in Audite vpon William Canynges ij chauntryes and the vicorye and the propters [procurators] with them. And aftir the seide Audyte is fynesshid, the Towne clerk to entre thaccompte of the same in a boke there, called Canynges liger, and there the Maire to receyve I noble, the toune clerk xx*d*., the swerdberer viij*d*., and the four Sergeauntez of the Maire xvi*d*.[3]

Among the wills proved in the Court of Husting of this period we find several in which land or tenements were left to specific persons on condition that a chantry should be maintained out of

[1] Associated Architectural Societies' *Reports*, XXXVII, p. 22.
[2] *Ricart's Kalendar*, ed. L. Toulmin Smith, p. 76. [3] *Ibid.* p. 79.

the profits, and containing the proviso that in case of failure to observe these terms the property should pass into other hands. In 1375, for example, William de Bathe bequeathed his tenement in Shoe Lane to the prioress and convent of Ankerwyke near Windsor, on condition that they maintain a chantry for the good of his soul, and the souls of others, and keep the said tenement in good repair; and on failing this after due admonition, "the said tenement is to go to the Prior and Convent of Westsmethefeld on the same terms; and if they should fail to carry out the conditions imposed, the same is to remain to the Dean and Chapter of S. Paul's".[1]

About the same time, the regulations that were drawn up for a chantry in St Martin's le Grand sought to provide against the same danger in another way. In this record it was laid down that "lest by long voidance of the chantry the souls of the deceased be defrauded of their due suffrages", the emoluments of the chantries during voidances shall "be collected by the two canons resident in the said chapel, or by one of them if two be not present, and be distributed publicly and of the knowledge of the choir to pious uses for the souls of the aforesaid, so that no benefit accrue to the dean from such voidance".[2] It is evident that the founder of this chantry clearly foresaw the temptation of the ecclesiastical body to leave it vacant and turn its revenues to their own uses, and though other founders expressed their fears less decidedly, the detailed prescriptions with regard to the exercise of patronage which we find in many foundation deeds were doubtless attempts to guard against the same evil.[3] The obligation of presenting a chantry priest within twenty days of the benefice's becoming void, or even within a shorter period, was frequently imposed, and it was often further provided that in case of failure to comply with this requirement the patronage should pass, for that turn, to other persons. In a deed of 1336, for example, by which Hugh de Wheatley established a chantry in the church of Hale, we read:

I ordain that the chaplain shall be presented to the bishop to be

[1] *Calendar of Wills proved in the Court of Husting, London*, ed. R.R. Sharpe, part ii, pp. 182–3.

[2] *Cal. Pat. Rolls*, 1367–70, p. 179.

[3] *Records of the Borough of Nottingham*, I, p. 132; *Cal. Pat. Rolls*, 1350–54, p. 74.

instituted, and that while I live I shall have the presentation, and after my death the rector of Great Hale shall present; and if he fail to present within eight days from the time of receiving notice of the vacancy, the presentation shall devolve upon the abbot and convent of Bardeney, the patrons of the church, and if they fail to present within eight days the collation shall devolve upon the bishop, and after other eight days the chapter shall provide a chaplain and if they cannot provide one, the right of presenting shall return to the rector.[1]

From the document relating to St Martin's just cited, we see also the founder's belief that his soul would suffer if the appointed number of masses were not said. The same view is expressed also in the precautions taken by many founders to see that the priest did not omit any of the masses which he was supposed to celebrate. In some cases he was required to pay a small fine for every mass omitted[2] and it was not uncommon to ordain that the chaplain should not spend a single night away from the town in which his chantry was situated, without having obtained the leave of the parish priest, or, in his absence, of one of the churchwardens.[3] Some founders were even more exacting, and required that their chaplains, when prevented by illness or other cause from personally celebrating the appointed services, should provide substitutes. For example, in the foundation deeds of the chantry for two priests which William de Amyas established in Nottingham in 1339, the rule is laid down that if either chaplain absent himself for more than eight days without reasonable cause, and without having put in his place another suitable chaplain to make the required celebrations, he should forthwith be deprived.[4]

But perhaps the most interesting evidence as to the importance attached to the saying of the appointed masses is contained in a remarkable entry on the Patent Rolls of 1368. From this we learn that at some previous date William Boteler of Canterbury had bequeathed his tenements in that city to his son Thomas and the heirs of his body, on condition that they should "find a chaplain to celebrate divine service daily in the church of St Andrew and a torch burning there at the time of masses—on

[1] Associated Architectural Societies' *Reports*, XXXVII, p. 61.
[2] *E.g. Calendar of the Manuscripts of the Dean and Chapter of Wells*, p. 459.
[3] *The Little Red Book of Bristol*, I, p. 220.
[4] *Records of the Borough of Nottingham*, I, pp. 132, 136, n. 1.

the failure of which condition the nearest heirs successively, and then the bailiffs of Canterbury, were to have power to enter therein". By 1368, Thomas had died without heir of his body, and the bailiffs of Canterbury were in possession of William Boteler's bequest, and were obtaining the king's confirmation of their grant of

> the said tenements to Simon de Burgh in fee so that he may fulfil the conditions laid down in the said will and find another chaplain to celebrate in that church as many masses as were omitted in the time of a late cessation of the said chantry by reason of the death of the said Thomas without heir of his body.[1]

The endowments of this chantry seem to have fallen into the hands of persons who held exceptionally conscientious views of their duty towards the souls of the dead; for nowhere else have I met with a provision for the saying of masses which had been previously omitted, while there is much evidence to show that the fears that many persons entertained lest their chantries should be neglected were far from groundless. As early as 1285, the second Statute of Westminster had laid down that if lands or rent which had been given for the support of a light, chantry, or other work of piety were turned to other uses, the grantor or his heirs might recover the alienated property.[2] Now, however medieval statutes may have been enforced, it is certain that they were not made to guard against hypothetical evils, but to remedy abuses which were already known to exist. It may, therefore, be safely assumed that when this statute was promulgated, the neglect of chantries and other works of piety by those who had been entrusted with their maintenance was well known. Moreover, all through the fourteenth century the complaint that chantries which had been appointed in religious houses had been allowed to cease, constantly recurs.

A charge to this effect was, as we have seen, brought against almost every monastery in whose affairs the king found it necessary to interfere, and still more important is the evidence of the following letter of the year 1345, preserved among the archives of the city of London, and translated by Riley in his *Memorials of London*:

To the Dean and Chapter of the Church of St Paul in London,

[1] *Cal. Pat. Rolls*, 1367–70, p. 170. [2] *Statutes of the Realm*, I, p. 92.

shew the Mayor, Aldermen, and Commonalty, of the same city, that whereas it is well known that many men and women of the City have devised in their testaments, and given in other ways, to the Dean and Chapter of the same church, and to their successors, many tenements and rents in the said city, for founding and maintaining diverse Chantries in the same church, and for offering up prayers and other devotions perpetually for their souls; as to the which many memorials remain with you, and also with ourselves, in our treasury at the Guildhall; and whereas we have fully understood, and also, do see it daily with our own eyes, when we pass by your Church of St Paul,—the which we do hold to be our Mother Church,—that there are but few Chaplains to sing there, in proportion to the Chantries which in the said church have been founded; to the great peril of your souls, who ought to oversee the said Chantries, maintain, and support the same; we do pray and request you, to the honour of God, and for the profit of the said church, and of yourselves and your successors, and the salvation of your souls, that you will cause such defaults to be amended and redressed in your time, that so the Chantries may be maintained, according to the wishes of the testators and donors thereof; you not having regard to the words of any person who shall wish to gainsay the said matter, but only for the honour of God and the salvation of your souls. And to the end that persons may have the greater feelings of devotion and may bestow alms, honours, and other bounty, upon your church aforesaid, let no person who holds a benefice or Chantry elsewhere, hold any Chantry in the same church; and then, only a single Chantry, at the which he may be personally in attendance, to do what shall thereunto pertain.[1]

Further evidence as to the neglect of chantries comes from legal records, in which we read of the recovery of property against corporations which had failed to maintain the chantries for which it had been granted.[2] A few of these cases have been recorded in the Year Books and in the Letter Books of the city of London, and it is probable that a search of the Plea Rolls would reveal many more.

Most of the neglected chantries of which we hear were those under the supervision of monastic or collegiate bodies, but occasionally, at least, lay trustees proved equally unfaithful. In 1363, John de Hatfield, senior, bequeathed to his son John, and certain other persons, parishioners of the church of St Benedict,

[1] H. T. Riley, *Memorials of London*, pp. 224–5.

[2] *E.g. Year Books*, 5 *Edward II* (Selden Soc.), pp. 128–9; *Year Books*, 15 *Edward III* (Rolls Series), pp. 448–9.

Gracechurch Street, a tenement and certain rents, in trust for the maintenance of a chantry in that church, with the proviso that in case of default the property should remain to the Mayor and Commonalty of London for the maintenance of London Bridge and of a chantry in the chapel of St Thomas the Martyr thereon.[1] What led to the discontinuance of this chantry, we do not know, but in 1394, Thomas, son and heir of John Hatfeld, senior, quitclaimed to the Mayor and Commonalty, and the wardens of London Bridge, this property "which had been seized by the said Mayor, etc., in default of the said chantry being maintained according to the terms of the will of the said John Hatfeld".[2]

The continuance of a chantry might also be threatened, through no fault of the patron, if the priest who had been presented obtained an additional benefice. This was apt to lead to non-residence, which in the case of some individuals was sanctioned, even by the popes. In 1402, for example, the pope granted an indult to Roger Melles, perpetual vicar in the church of Wells,

> who holds also a chantry in the chapel of St Mary the Virgin in the cemetery of the church of Wollavyngton in the diocese of Wells, both without cure, and who is bound by oath to say in the said chapel the *Placebo* and *Dirige*, the canonical hours, and other prayers and commendations for the souls of its founders and other faithful departed—to say such hours, prayers and commendations in the said church of Wells or elsewhere, to take the fruits etc. of the said chantry as if he resided in the said chapel, and not to be bound to say the said hours etc. there, nor to reside.[3]

It may of course be argued that by this indult Roger Melles was excused only from the duty of personal residence at Woolavington, and that as the duties of a vicar of Wells Cathedral were probably not incompatible with those of a chantry priest little harm was done. This is no doubt true in theory, but if Roger had remained at Woolavington, any serious failure to fulfil his obligations would have been quickly noticed by the vicar or the parishioners, while at Wells, where few persons were likely to know precisely what were his duties as chantry priest of Wool-

[1] *Calendar of Wills proved in the Court of Husting, London*, part ii, p. 79.
[2] *Calendar of Letter Books of the City of London*, Letter Book H, p. 411.
[3] *Cal. Papal Letters*, v, p. 519.

avington, and where there would be no one to see that they were performed, the sense of obligation which his own conscience might or might not impose must have been almost the only authority to which, in his capacity of chantry priest, he was subject. At any rate, it is certain that founders feared the harm which might come to their chantries through their chaplains holding other benefices at the same time. This is shown clearly by the precautions which some founders took to prevent their chantries from being held by pluralists. Thus, part of the oath which the priest, who served Richard le Spicer's chantry at Bristol, was required to take on his admission was "quod nullum beneficium cum cura vel sine cura sine resignacione dicte cantarie occupabit, sed infra mensem post adeptum beneficium dicte cantarie palam et publice resignabit".[1] The evils which this and similar oaths were intended to prevent were, at least, only temporary, and on the death of a negligent chantry priest, a successor who would reside and conform to the regulations might be presented, but many chantries were allowed to cease for ever. The history of one of these may be learned from a papal letter of 1402. This was issued in response to a petition from the master and scholars of Michaelhouse, Cambridge, stating that

> formerly the late John Ilberg *alias* Horwode, then rector of All Saints', Ikelingham, in the diocese of Norwich, instituted in the said college two scholars to study, and one chaplain to celebrate masses of the Blessed Virgin, assigning certain yearly rents for their sustentation;

and adding that

> the said rents, through the malice of the times, afterwards became so diminished that such scholars and chaplain could not and cannot be sustained therewith, wherefore for some time past there has been and is no such chaplain, nor are the said fruits likely to increase.

In response to this petition, the pope granted that if the facts were as stated the college should not be bound to keep such chaplain and that the portion of fruits concerning him should be applied to the use of the two scholars; enjoining, however, that if this were carried out there should be in each mass of the Blessed Virgin which was celebrated in the college a special commemoration of the said John, by a collect for the welfare of his soul.[2]

[1] *The Little Red Book of Bristol*, I, p. 219.
[2] *Cal. Papal Letters*, V, p. 585.

From this we see that when the income from the benefaction became insufficient for all the charges it had been intended to meet, the first economy that was adopted appears to have been the abandonment of the chantry. Presumably one, instead of two scholars, might have been kept and the chaplain retained, or all the requirements might have been satisfied by ordering that one of the scholars should be a priest and should undertake the duties of the chaplain. For priests maintained themselves at the universities by serving chantries while engaged in their studies. From a latitudinarian point of view the arrangement which the pope allowed may seem perfectly satisfactory, but when we remember the great importance which the men of that age attached to the celebration of masses for the dead, we cannot but feel that the master and scholars were guilty of a most selfish breach of trust. It may be urged in extenuation of this act that according to modern canon law, when the pope dissolves a chantry in this manner, he gives to the souls of those for whom it was founded all the spiritual benefits which they should have received had the masses been duly celebrated. No authoritative pronouncement of this doctrine, however, was made during the Middle Ages, and there is no evidence that the matter was even discussed during our period. A medieval man, therefore, who saw a chantry come to an end, even though the cessation was allowed by the highest ecclesiastical authority, may well have feared the consequences to the dead founder's soul.

A chantry might, of course, be discontinued through no fault of the patron's but merely because, as prices rose, no priest could be found who would serve for the small stipend which the endowments provided. Thus in 1364, Thomas de Garwynton obtained a licence to grant in mortmain to

> the hospital of St John the Baptist, Northgate, in the suburb of Canterbury, 32 acres of land, 16*s*. 5½*d*. of rent and a rent of 8 cocks and 19 hens, in Welle by Canterbury, whereof a chantry called 'Lukedale' of the patronage of the said Thomas, was founded and endowed of ancient time which no chaplain cares to serve because the land and rents are insufficient for the sustenance of a chaplain, and for that cause they have come into his hands as the patron.[1]

Whether the members of the hospital who received this grant

[1] *Cal. Pat. Rolls*, 1364–67, p. 8.

undertook to perform any works of piety for the souls of those who had been commemorated in the chantry does not appear, and without knowledge on that point, the patron's conduct cannot fairly be judged, but if the statements made in the licence were true the cessation of the chantry must be attributed to economic causes over which he had no control.

It is impossible to say whether, during this period, many chantries came to an end owing to the inadequacy of their endowments as, generally speaking, the records mention the insufficiency of their revenues only when they were being turned to other uses, or when they were being augmented in order that the chantry might continue; and, in some cases, when a priest could no longer be supported, the patron may have resumed possession of the property without seeking a licence to convert it to other pious uses. Some founders were fortunate in discovering the inadequacy of the provision they had at first made, in time for themselves or those personally interested in their welfare to add to the original grant. In 1331, for example, Laurence de Dunolmo, executor of the will of John de Ellerker, obtained licence for the alienation in mortmain of fifty shillings in rent in Newcastle-upon-Tyne to a chaplain celebrating divine service daily in the church of St Nicholas there, for the souls of John de Ellerker and his wife, "a messuage and 20s. in rent alienated for the sustenance of such chaplain by the said John with the late king's licence having proved insufficient for the purpose".[1] In the foregoing document, Laurence de Dunolmo was probably doing no more than carrying out the terms of John de Ellerker's will. But towards the end of the period here considered, we find a number of licences for alienations of property with a view to re-establishing or rendering more secure chantries which either had ceased or were in danger of being discontinued, and the persons who made these grants appear to have been acting quite independently of the original founders. Help of this kind was probably given from a generous desire that the founder, who may have been a kinsman or friend, should not lose the masses for which he had endeavoured to provide, and those who undertook this charitable work probably did so the more readily because of the opportunity it offered of securing at the same time

[1] *Cal. Pat. Rolls*, 1330–34, p. 54.

some benefit for their own souls. An excellent illustration of what might be done in such a case is afforded by the following item from the Patent Roll of 1374.

On the petition of the king's clerk, John de Ravenser, praying that whereas a chantry of one chaplain lately founded in the town of Helhowe and endowed with certain possessions and rents in the town of Waltham, is almost desolate and destroyed owing to the poorness of the profits and its distance from its possessions, so that no chaplain has cared to serve it for long, and he, with the king's licence and the authority and assent of the diocesan of the place and of those interested, purposes to transfer the chantry to the church of Waltham so that the chaplain to be ordained to celebrate at the altar of St Nicholas in the said church for the soul of the founder of the chantry shall have the original rents and possessions thereof, and desires to augment the same with certain lands and possessions in order that he may participate in so great a work of piety, the king will be pleased to grant him licence to alienate in mortmain two messuages, 24 acres of land and 8 acres of meadow in Waltham to the said chaplain to celebrate divine service daily in the church of Waltham for the soul of the founder of the first chantry, and for the safe estate of Richard de Ravenser, clerk, and of the said John, and for their souls after their death, and the souls of their fathers, mothers and benefactors.[1]

It is possible that when the endowments of a chantry proved insufficient, it might be saved from entire extinction by a reduction in the number of masses which the chaplain was bound to celebrate. Recourse to this expedient seems to have been very rare, but we know that it was sometimes contemplated, even at the time when a chantry was being established. Dr Heepe has found several examples of this, and he cites some cases in which the chaplain was required to say as many masses in each week, up to the number of seven, as he received marks in the year.[2] I have found no English document that records so definite an arrangement, but a similar idea is expressed in an agreement of 1384, by which the dean and chapter of Lincoln, in return for a grant of certain lands and tenements, undertook to provide a chaplain to celebrate daily for the souls of Walter de Ounesby and others,

that a sufficient salary shall be received from the dean and chapter out

[1] *Cal. Pat. Rolls*, 1370–74, p. 410.

[2] *Die Organisation der Altarpfründen an den Pfarrkirchen der Stadt Braunschweig im Mittelalter*, p. 52.

of those lands and tenements of Ounesby and Croketon which formerly were Walter's, as may be agreed between the dean and chapter and the chaplain and his successors; so that the chantry for their souls may in no wise cease for ever; namely, as long as and whenever the lands and tenements shall suffice to bear the charges laid upon them. So nevertheless that whenever they shall not suffice, the dean and chapter shall cause service to be celebrated for the souls aforesaid in proportion to the quantity and portion of their value, or distribute the [rents] in other works of piety, according to their discretion, so that always and whenever and as often as they shall suffice, the dean and chapter shall be by all means bound to provide the chaplain for the souls aforesaid.[1]

Another expedient is suggested in a licence of 1391. This states that on his last visitation Robert, bishop of London, had found

that the chantries, hereinafter named in St Paul's cathedral church were of such small value that they could not be conveniently served individually, and that many were held incompatibly with other benefices with cure of souls requiring personal residence,[2] and on account of the urgent need of ministers in the said church, which was more than usually destitute, it was then proposed with the assent of the chapter and all concerned to unite and incorporate the same.[3]

The document from which the above quotation is taken was a grant of the king's assent to the plan which the bishop had suggested. The chantries which were to be affected, with the annual income of each, are given at the end of the letter. They provide, in all, for fifty-four priests. The annual value of some of them was indeed small, several being worth no more than forty or fifty shillings, but a considerable number would seem to have been so well endowed that it is surprising to find them in this list, four chaplains receiving nine marks, one ten marks and two twelve marks.[4] Precisely what steps were taken after the licence had been procured, I have not been able to discover. It is fairly clear that the souls of the numerous founders were not provided

[1] Associated Architectural Societies' *Reports*, XXXVII, p. 78.

[2] This evidence confirms the statement in *Piers the Plowman*:

"Persones and parisch prestes playneth to heore bisschops,
That heore parisch hath ben pore seththe the pestilence tyme,
And asketh leue and lycence at Londun to dwelle,
To singe ther for simonye for seluer is swete". A, Prologue, 80.

[3] *Cal. Pat. Rolls*, 1388–92, p. 421.

[4] *Ibid.* 1388–92, pp. 421–2.

for by a single chantry of one or more priests, but in several cases two or three chantries were probably combined to form one, served by a single priest. This I infer from the fact that in the certificates of 1 Edward VI,[1] relating to St Paul's, several chantries are described as having been founded by two persons, each of whom, according to the 1391 list, had originally founded a chantry of his own.

Some founders, it would seem, endeavoured to secure their chantries against any likelihood of cessation owing to lack of funds by providing that all who contributed towards their support should share in the spiritual benefits. The licence issued in 1366, for instance, by which Master Robert de Beverlaco was permitted to found a chantry, stated that the priest was to celebrate for the soul of Robert and a number of persons mentioned by name "and all others helping in the sustenance of the said chaplain".[2] It is noteworthy also that some ecclesiastics included their successors and their spiritual superiors among those for whom their chantry priests were to pray. The most interesting example of this practice that has come to my notice is an item on the Patent Roll of 1330, by which Geoffrey de Edenham, king's clerk, late vicar of the church of Woodhorn, in the diocese of Durham, obtained a licence to grant in mortmain to Luke de Periers, now vicar of that church, a messuage in Newcastle-upon-Tyne,

> to find a chantry in the said church and in the chapels thereto annexed every day in the week, for the souls of the said Geoffrey and Luke, and their predecessors and successors, vicars of Wodehorn, and for the souls of Richard de Kellawe sometime bishop of Durham, and Lewis de Bello Monte, now bishop, and of their predecessors and successors in the see.[3]

From the fact that the messuage whose revenues were to support this chantry was granted to the then vicar of Woodhorn, it seems most likely that the vicar of the church for the time being would have the patronage; when, therefore, Geoffrey de Edenham desired that all his predecessors and successors should be remembered in his chantry, he may have done so from a genuine affection for the parish, and a wish that all who held the same

[1] Dugdale, *Saint Paul's Cathedral*, pp. 380 ff.
[2] *Cal. Pat. Rolls*, 1364–67, pp. 233, 234.
[3] *Ibid.* 1327–30, p. 552.

office should share in the spiritual advantages of the chantry, but he may also have hoped that all the future vicars of Woodhorn, being thus made recipients of the benefits of the chantry, would execute their trust more faithfully for having a personal interest in its continuance. To the same motive may be attributed the inclusion of the bishops of Durham, who of course had the right of visiting and of instituting to the chantries in their see, and who might be expected to watch over those in which their own souls were specially commended with even greater care than their official responsibilities required. But while the patron was frequently, and the diocesan was often, given a share in the prayers of a chantry priest, it is surprising to find how often members of the royal family were included. Without having compiled exact statistics on this point, I believe it would be safe to say that the king, his progenitors and heirs were to be commended in the masses of at least half of the chantries for the endowment of which licences were obtained. The inclusion of the king among the beneficiaries of so many chantries was probably due to a variety of causes. Courtiers, both clerics and laymen, were no doubt often sincerely attached to Edward III, whom many saw as the founder of their fortunes, and in whose pleasures and adventures many had borne a part; for such persons to direct that their chantry priests should pray for the souls of the king and queen and their heirs was natural enough, and with many who owed nothing directly to the sovereign, his inclusion was probably a general expression of patriotism. But more selfish motives may also have existed in the minds of founders, since the promise of prayers for the king and his descendants might secure his good will towards a new chantry and so enable the alienator to obtain his licence on more favourable terms.

These remarks are not intended to reflect discredit on the characters of our medieval ancestors. But an impartial student is bound to point out the possible advantages that might be gained by naming certain persons among the beneficiaries of a chantry; and considering the many dangers that threatened the continuance of even seemingly securely founded chantries, those who endeavoured to safeguard them by offering spiritual advantages to the persons on whom their existence might in the future depend, seem hardly deserving of censure. It is clear, moreover, that generous motives were in the minds of the great majority of founders. This is shown by the fact that the commonest requirements were that the chaplain should celebrate not only for the founder's soul, but for those of his family, friends, and benefactors, and—the phrase is used so constantly that it seems almost common form—for all the faithful departed. Moreover, the records contain a number of instances of exceptionally disinterested provisions which, in our general estimate of the men of those times, help to atone for the cases of unusual selfishness. One founder of a chantry, Thomas de Sibthorp, a king's clerk, obtained, in 1332, a licence to grant certain property in mortmain to a chaplain who should celebrate divine service daily for his soul and the souls of his parishioners.[1]

By another licence, issued in 1330, Henry de Cantuaria was allowed to alienate in mortmain four messuages to the master and brethren of the hospital of poor priests at Canterbury, to find a chaplain to celebrate divine service daily, "for the peace of the church and realm, and for the souls of the said Henry, his parents, and benefactors".[2] One further instance of a chantry founded for an exceptionally generous object deserves to be quoted. Among the mortmain licences of 1351 is one authorizing the transfer of certain lands and rents to three chaplains, to celebrate divine service daily, two in Reculver church and one in the chapel of Hythe annexed to the same church, "for the good estate of the king and the peace and tranquillity of England, for the soul of the king after he is dead and for the souls of those who have died on account of his wars".[3] Thus, in some cases at least, it must have been felt that the community, and not merely the founder and his kindred, benefited by the prayers which the chantry priest offered, and it has been asserted also that the chantries rendered other services to the parishes in which they were established.

Rock, for example, claimed that "a weekly dole to the poor was usually provided for by most founders of chantries",[4] but he cites only one example in support of this statement, the chantry certificate of Sir Christopher Clark, "chauntre prest" of Hedcron

[1] *Cal. Pat. Rolls*, 1330–34, p. 376. [2] *Ibid.* 1330–34, pp. 10, 11.
[3] *Ibid.* 1350–54, p. 118.
[4] *The Church of Our Fathers*, III, p. 85, n. 97.

in Kent, who was bound to distribute seven pence weekly to seven poor persons. Other instances of this practice were probably known to Rock, but to say that provision for a weekly distribution to the poor was a usual part of the regulations of a chantry is, at the least, a serious exaggeration. In the mortmain licences concerning chantries of Edward III's reign, though alms-giving is mentioned fairly frequently, indications of a weekly distribution are extremely rare, and the impression which this evidence conveys is confirmed by all the actual foundation deeds that I have been able to examine. From these records, as from the Patent Rolls, we learn that, in the majority of cases, when provision was made for alms, it was not for a weekly, but for an annual distribution on the day of the founder's obit. For example, in the regulations of the chantry which William Everard and his wife Elizabeth established at Christchurch, Twynham, it was laid down that the chaplain should distribute yearly "on the days of the obit and anniversary of William and Elizabeth, to each of sixty poor persons in the town of Twynham, bread, ale, and companage to the value of 1*d*."[1] Doubtless these occasional gifts came as a welcome relief to many poor persons, who must have rejoiced when they heard the crier going through the town calling upon the people to pray for the soul of some deceased person, the eve of whose anniversary it was, and thus giving notice that the anniversary with its customary gifts of food and drink would be kept on the morrow. But the amount which each person received on these occasions was usually too small really to better his condition, though doubtless affording the kind of temporary satisfaction which in modern times is given by the Christmas dinners to the poor which many charitable associations supply. This, except in a few cases, appears to have been all the material assistance to the poor which the chantries provided.

Those chantries to which schools were attached were, no doubt, of great service to the community, but though Leach mentions a few chantry schools founded before or during our period,[2] they were still rare, and throughout Edward III's reign it was customary to require only spiritual duties of the chantry priest.

[1] *Cal. Pat. Rolls*, 1340–43, p. 387.
[2] *The Schools of Medieval England*, pp. 197, 199, 200, 210.

It has been affirmed by some writers that these priests were bound to assist the incumbents of the churches in which their chantries were situated. In a sense this is true, but unless the position is very carefully defined such a statement may easily be misleading. On admission to the chantry, the priest was commonly required to take an oath of obedience to the rector or vicar.[1] This probably meant only that in matters relating to his duties as a chaplain he was placed under the supervision of the parish priest. Thus, according to many chantry regulations, he might not absent himself from the town without the leave of the parson, or, in his absence, the leave of one of the churchwardens. The chaplain, moreover, was almost invariably required to be present in the choir during the celebration of the parochial mass, and to say all the canonical hours with the parish priest,[2] and, at a later period at least, he was obliged to read the lessons, epistles and gospels, at high mass, if the parson desired him to do so.[3] This, however, appears to be the full amount of assistance which he was expected to render to the parish priest. In fact, one of the principal points to be laid down in the regulations of chantries was that the chaplains should not usurp any part of the functions of the rectors or vicars, nor receive payments from the parishioners.[4] The income of most parish priests, it must be remembered, depended in no small measure on the customary offerings made at baptisms, funerals and other ecclesiastical ceremonies. Consequently, they jealously guarded their right to administer all sacraments lest they or their successors should lose the profits or any part of them. When, as must often have happened, the relations between the chantry priest and his rector were friendly, the former, whose duties were always comparatively light, may from time to time have performed some task which, strictly speaking, belonged to the rector. But such assistance when it was given depended entirely on the chaplain's good will and the parish priest's confidence in him, and formed no part of the duties to which he was bound. These, as a rule, were confined to

[1] "Constitutions of Simon Mepham", printed in Sir H. Spelman's *Concilia*, II, p. 501.

[2] Spelman, *Concilia*, II, p. 437.

[3] J. Johnson, *English Canons*, part ii, p. 501.

[4] Spelman, *Concilia*, pp. 436–7; see also foundation deeds in *The Little Red Book of Bristol*.

the celebration of the daily mass, and frequently also of the office of the dead, and participation in the appointed services of the parish church. The chaplain must, therefore, have had at his disposal almost as much time as the vicar or rector had for the performance of the manifold tasks associated with his office, and thus he probably enjoyed a greater amount of leisure than any other class of medieval men who were obliged to earn their own living. Of how the chantry priests employed this leisure, we know little. During our period nothing appears to have been said officially on this subject. In 1444, Archbishop Kemp exhorted the chaplains to devote their leisure to study instead of spending it in taverns and other unlawful places,[1] but there is nothing to indicate whether the advice was followed.

Apart from the performance of the church services, the only responsibilities with which the chantry priest was likely to be burdened were the care of his chapel and its ornaments, and of the property from which his income was derived. For example, the priest who served the chantry of Richard de Welles, at Bristol, was required, within fifteen days of his admission, to make an inventory of all the books and other things belonging to his chapel, and to keep them safely, and in good repair, and he was also obliged to repair the tenements in Bristol from whose rents this chantry was maintained.[2] Another founder of a chantry, also in Bristol, William le Spicer by name, provided for the maintenance of the buildings on which it depended by ordaining that each year the chaplain should pay to the wardens of the church of St Nicholas, where the chantry was, twenty shillings, "qui remanebunt in eorum manibus et custodia ad sustentandum et reparandum tenementa, shopas et solarium suprascripta cum necesse fuerit".[3]

So business-like an arrangement as this, however, seems to have been rare, and as a rule the chaplain was merely required to keep the buildings in repair on pain of losing his benefice.

Such obligations were light in comparison with those that the ordinary parish priest had to undertake. For the latter, besides keeping his house and the chancel of the church in repair, must

[1] Johnson, *English Canons*, part ii, p. 501.

[2] *The Little Red Book of Bristol*, I, p. 214.

[3] *Ibid.* p. 220.

exercise hospitality and pay synodals and other dues. One might, therefore, expect to find that the chantry priest was paid at a lower rate than the incumbent of a parochial living. Certainly there were no chantries equal in wealth to the more valuable rectories, but valuable rectories, when they had not been appropriated, were likely to be held by non-resident clergy who paid comparatively small salaries to the priests whom they appointed to take their places. It may therefore be doubted whether the income of the chantry priests was less than that of the majority of those who were actually exercising cure of souls in the parishes. To compare their salaries is, however, extremely difficult. For just as the income of the parish priest consisted largely of tithes and other payments in kind, which must have varied from year to year, and the exact value of which, even for a single year, cannot now be ascertained, so provision for the support of the chantry priest was often made by a grant to him, or to those by whom he was to be paid, of a specified amount of arable land, meadow, pasture and wood, whose annual profits it is quite impossible to determine. Frequently, nevertheless, the chantry priest's stipend consisted of a fixed money rent, and from these a general impression of the customary rates of payment may be obtained. Some founders seem to have believed or hoped that four marks would suffice for the chaplain's salary, but the amounts most commonly granted for this purpose were five or six marks. The frequency with which these sums occur indicates a widespread belief that it would make an adequate provision for a chaplain's needs, and the founders may well have been helped towards this estimate by the fact that five marks had long been fixed as the minimum salary which a parochial vicar ought to receive. But as the serving of chantries was largely a matter of private concern, the founder was, until late in the Middle Ages, left free to grant what stipend he thought fit. In most cases, no doubt, the founder endeavoured to allow a suitable amount; for the chantry's continuance was too closely connected with the eternal welfare of his own soul for him to have been under much temptation to economize at its expense. At any rate, there seems to have been no danger that the chantry priests would, as a class, be underpaid as the vicars of an earlier period had been; for when, at length, the ecclesiastical authorities began to intervene in this matter, it was to protect the interests of others than the chaplains.

The first attempt to regulate the wages of chantry priests was made in 1347, when William la Zouche, then archbishop of York, issued a decree limiting the wages of all chaplains,[1] whether they were serving in parishes, chantries, chapels, or other benefices, to six marks a year, but explaining that this was not intended to alter existing agreements.[2] Two years later, when the pestilence had greatly increased the scarcity of priests, the regulation of chaplains' wages became a matter of serious concern to both the civil and the ecclesiastical authorities. The consequent legislation on this subject has, however, been so fully discussed by Miss B. H. Putnam[3] that it is only necessary to say here that throughout the reign of Edward III the wages of parochial chaplains were limited to six marks and those of chantry priests to five marks, though legislation of 1378 raised the maximum stipend for both classes by two marks.

It is clear from the evidence which Miss Putnam has brought together that the necessity for such measures was a matter on which many if not all sections of the community, except, of course, the chaplains themselves, were agreed; and for this there were two important reasons. Many persons of all the more prosperous classes were, or hoped to become, the founders of perpetual chantries, or at least intended to provide in their wills for the hire of priests to sing masses for them during a specified period. All such persons would naturally feel a strong personal interest in preventing this pious work from becoming too expensive. But a more serious and a less selfish motive also had great influence. During the fourteenth century many parochial livings tended to become poorer, and at the same time the founding of chantries went on rapidly, and after the pestilence the number of priests available to serve either was greatly reduced. The efforts to keep the chantry priests' salaries at exactly the same amount as before the general rise in prices appear unreasonable, for some alteration was necessary if their real wages were not to fall far below what they had been at the

[1] "Chaplain" is here used in its ordinary medieval sense as designating any hired priest.

[2] Spelman, *Concilia*, p. 603.

[3] *American Historical Review*, XXI, pp. 12–32.

beginning of the century. But if there were not enough priests for all the benefices, there was a real danger that the poorer parochial livings and the chaplaincies with cure of souls would be deserted if the service of chantries were allowed to become too lucrative. This danger was clearly recognized. La Zouche tried to meet it by ordering that chantries and other benefices without cure of souls should not be filled till the parishes had been supplied with priests; and the decrees allowing chaplains having cure of souls to receive one mark more than those who merely served chantries were made with the same object in view.[1] It is certain, however, that many persons who founded chantries between 1350 and the end of the reign endowed their chaplains with incomes far exceeding five marks; provisions for stipends of eight, nine or ten marks occurring not infrequently. One of the richest chantries of the period was that which Edmund Blanket, a burgess of Bristol, founded on behalf of himself and his family. The tenements in Bristol, from the rent of which all expenses connected with the chantry were to be met, he assigned to the vicar and churchwardens of the church of St Stephen, in that town, who were to keep the buildings in repair, to find a missal, chalice, bread, wine and all other things necessary for the celebration of masses; and to pay the priest for his salary nine marks at the least. It was, perhaps, necessary for the protection of the fortunate priest who obtained this benefice that the foundation deed should contain a very unusual clause forbidding his removal by false suggestion and unless he were proved guilty of some grave offence.[2] Here we have a definite case of a chantry priest whose income would equal or even surpass that of many vicars and rectors, and that there can have been little difference between the profits received by many chantry priests and the incumbents of parish churches is attested by the very frequent exchanges of benefices between priests of these classes.

Financially, then, there was often little to choose between serving a chantry and a parish with cure of souls, and a poor parish priest might even better his condition by resigning and accepting a chantry. When to this consideration is added the comparative freedom from responsibility, and the great amount

[1] Spelman, *Concilia*, p. 603; *Rot. Parl.* II, p. 271.
[2] *The Little Red Book of Bristol*, I, p. 225.

of leisure which the chantry priest enjoyed, it is not surprising if, not infrequently, a poor parson would, as Chaucer complained—

> Leet his sheep encombred in the myre,
> And ran to London, un-to seynt Poules,
> To seken him a chaunterie for soules.

There remain for our consideration the question of what chances a priest would have of obtaining such preferment, and the closely allied problem of the influence of the Black Death on the founding of chantries. The answers to these questions should depend very largely on the numbers of chantries that were being founded year by year, but that is a matter on which precise information cannot be obtained, as there is no means of discovering exactly how many chantries were established within any given period. Nevertheless, since more satisfactory records are not available, something may be learned from the mortmain licences, without which no chantry could receive permanent endowments.

It must be remembered, however, that the obtaining of a licence for an alienation in mortmain was only one of the preliminaries to endowing a chantry and does not prove that the grant was actually made. Probably some persons who obtained licences never carried them out, and others contented themselves in the end with a less ambitious foundation than is described in the original licence. Thus in 1331, John de Trippelow, a chaplain, procured a licence to grant in mortmain eight messuages and eight acres of land in and near Cambridge to the prioress and convent of St Radegund's to find a chaplain to celebrate divine service daily in their church for the souls of John and his ancestors.[1] But when John de Trippelow actually conveyed this property to the convent all that they promised to do for him was to celebrate thirty masses a year in their church for the souls of him and his parents, "and to celebrate his anniversary as is done in the case of a nun deceased".[2] As the value of the property granted to St Radegund's is not given, it is impossible to decide whether this change was due to its being insufficient to support a chaplain, or whether John de Trippe-

[1] *Cal. Pat. Rolls*, 1330–34, p. 99.
[2] A. Gray, *The Priory of St Radegund, Cambridge*, p. 85.

low was accepting fewer masses merely in order that the convent might derive more profit from his gift. This is the only case I have so far discovered in which the alienator of property agreed to accept fewer masses than were specified in his mortmain licence, but the actual foundation deeds that I have been able to consult are few in comparison with the great number of mortmain licences; and it may well be that if more of the former could be examined, other cases similar to that of John de Trippelow would appear. The possibility that some alienations, which were intended to establish chantries, in reality procured some lesser spiritual benefit must, therefore, always be borne in mind.

Moreover, the language of the records themselves is often too indefinite to show clearly whether licence was being obtained to found a new chantry or only to increase the revenues of one that already existed.

But, although, for these reasons, the numbers of chantries that were being founded cannot be ascertained, the tendency to endow them may still be traced through the mortmain licences. I have, therefore, prepared the following table showing the number of licences which, according to the Patent Rolls, were issued in each year of Edward III's reign to sanction the granting of land or rent to chantries.

The figures have the effect of confirming one generally accepted belief, and of correcting another. They show that during the reign of Edward III the number of chantries that were endowed was, when the smallness of the population is considered, very great. But when we enquire in what years were the licences for this purpose most numerous, we find that they were not, as has commonly been supposed, the years that followed the pestilence, but the early years of Edward's reign. The largest numbers of licences were issued in 1334 (forty), 1345 (forty-one), and 1349 (forty), and from the beginning of the reign to the last-named date there were ten years in which the number was over thirty, but in no year after 1349 do as many as thirty appear. Moreover, between 1327 and 1349, there were only two years in which the licences for alienations to chantries numbered less than twenty—there being seventeen in 1339 and eighteen in 1348—while in the period which followed the first appearance of the pestilence, the number of licences fell below twenty on twenty-one occasions.

If the issue of licences in periods of ten years is examined, it will be seen that the highest number belonged to the first decade of the reign and that the number was in each succeeding ten years steadily diminished, until, in the last ten years, only half as many licences were issued as in the period 1327 to 1336.

Alienations in Mortmain

Year	Licences	Year	Licences
1327	27	1353	19
1328	39	1354	16
1329	35	1355	7
1330	33	1356	17 (220)
1331	34	1357	7
1332	34	1358	17
1333	28	1359	14
1334	40	1360	16
1335	25	1361	25
1336	29 (324)	1362	29
1337	27	1363	16
1338	32	1364	17
1339	17	1365	13
1340	29	1366	23 (177)
1341	21	1367	8
1342	22	1368	15
1343	28	1369	19
1344	31	1370	17
1345	41	1371	28
1346	20 (268)	1372	7
1347	25	1373	13
1348	18	1374	15
1349	40	1375	14
1350	27	1376	13
1351	27	1377	6 (155)
1352	24		1144

If this evidence is a trustworthy indication of what was going on, it must be concluded that the chantries had reached their greatest popularity well before the first appearance in England of the Black Death; and this conclusion is strengthened by the fact that the constitution of William la Zouche, the first document in which it is suggested that the large number of chantries constituted a danger to the parishes, was issued in 1347, a year before the pestilence first reached this country. Why it has been generally supposed that the founding of chantries was increased by the plague is easy to see. The greatness and suddenness of the calamity might be expected to cause many hitherto careless persons to take serious thought for the welfare of their souls, which would result in the establishment of chantries. But the scarcity of priests, which the plague caused, made it possible for the survivors to demand higher wages than ever before, while the general impoverishment would make the founding of new chantries exceptionally difficult, and thus, as the figures given above suggest, the effect of the plague was to discourage, rather than to stimulate, the endowment of chantries.

CHAPTER V

APPROPRIATION OF PARISH CHURCHES

ONE further subject with which the Statute of Mortmain is concerned remains to be considered. This is the appropriation of parish churches. For since in England, advowsons were regarded as temporal property within the cognizance of the lay courts, the Statute of Mortmain was as much concerned with the church's acquisition of advowsons and tithes as of land or rent. No ecclesiastical body, therefore, could legally acquire an advowson unless a licence for the alienation in mortmain had been obtained. Moreover, when a church was appropriated and a monastery or other corporation became its rector, it would not again become vacant, and the king would thus lose the right of presenting to the rectory, which otherwise would have been his, whenever the church fell void while the advowson was in his hands; consequently, even when the would-be appropriators already held the patronage of a church, they could not convert its revenues to their own uses without obtaining letters patent sanctioning the appropriation.

Those who attempted to appropriate a church without royal licence ran the risk of losing its revenues altogether, for the punishment for this offence was forfeiture of the advowson; and if this law was enforced and the king's presentee was admitted to the rectory, the appropriation was, of course, dissolved. In practice, offenders of this kind were often pardoned and allowed to retain their churches, but to procure such a pardon probably involved greater difficulties and expenses than would have been needed to obtain the neglected licence. In these circumstances, the first step taken towards the appropriation of a church was commonly the procuring of a royal licence. It is true that in a number of instances a papal bull granting an appropriation was issued before the appropriators had obtained the king's assent, but its execution was probably delayed until after the royal licence had been granted. For example, in 1345, the monastery of Newburgh obtained a papal licence to appropriate the church of Owston,[1] the royal licence was granted in 1346,[2] and the first attempt to carry out the appropriation appears to have been made in 1348.[3] But, in general, those who wished to possess their churches without fear of molestation by the secular authorities, represented locally by the vigilant escheator, probably followed the strictly legal course, and began by obtaining a royal licence.

That these licences were necessary has been generally recognized, but what has not been observed is that they often contain a great deal more than a mere licence to appropriate, and that facts which do not appear in the ecclesiastical records are frequently to be found in these letters of the royal chancery.

The first point to be considered here concerns the general position of the papacy with regard to English appropriations, and is suggested by a comparison of the numbers of licences issued by the Royal and the Papal Chanceries. It is well known that according to canon law a church should be appropriated and the vicarage ordained by the bishop in whose diocese it was situated, but it has often been assumed that in practice this was not enough, and that an appropriating body which wished to be secure in the possession of any church would obtain a papal bull authorizing or confirming the appropriation. On this assumption, the number of churches mentioned in the Calendars of Papal Letters and Petitions as appropriated with the pope's assent has been regarded as approximately the number that was actually appropriated. Dr Hartridge has indeed recognized that statistics based on the Papal Registers are "under-estimates of the real total of appropriations that were going on", but when comparing the numbers of appropriations that were made about the time of the first appearance of the Black Death and a century later, he says that the statistics based on the appropriations in the Papal Registers are a thoroughly reliable guide as to proportion. His conclusion, however, seems to take no account of an important change in the attitude of the papacy towards appropriations. This change and its consequences must now be briefly examined.

During the half century of Edward III's reign the number of

[1] *Cal. Papal Letters*, III, p. 216. [2] *Cal. Pat. Rolls*, 1345–48, p. 146.
[3] *Cal. Papal Letters*, III, p. 347.

churches for the appropriation of which royal licences were issued was 539, while the appropriations which were granted or confirmed by the popes of the same period were about a hundred and forty. This difference is too great to be entirely explained by the fact that in most cases the obtaining of the royal licence was only the first step towards an appropriation, and that the parties concerned frequently went no further, and suggests that at that time many churches must have been appropriated without papal authority, and this view is confirmed by an examination of the contemporary episcopal registers. For example, of the twenty churches which John de Grandisson, bishop of Exeter from 1327 to 1369, appropriated, only three were commanded or confirmed by the pope. To discover exactly how many appropriations were made without recourse to Rome would, especially while many episcopal registers remain unprinted, be a task of great difficulty, and though it might produce interesting results, in showing the practice of individual bishops in this matter, would not alter the general conclusion that during most of our period papal authority was obtained in only a minority of cases.

If an appropriation was favoured by the bishop and other local authorities, and if no exceptional circumstances stood in the way of their action or rendered its legality doubtful, papal assistance seems to have been unnecessary, and in the majority of cases it was probably not sought. But the appropriation of many churches was hindered by unusual difficulties, to overcome which recourse to Rome was the surest, if not the only means. The Calendars of Papal Letters and Petitions make it clear that the pope's intervention was often obtained in order to overcome the opposition of the diocesan authorities, or to prevent them from exacting what seemed excessive compensation for the losses which they would sustain. Thus in 1347, Queen Isabella petitioned the pope for the appropriation to Tupholme Abbey of the church of Stretton, near Randeley, "notwithstanding that the diocesan and archdeacon assert that during its voidance certain parts of its rents and profits belong to them".[1] In a number of instances, also, more than one papal mandate was issued before an appropriation was carried out, and in some of these cases, though the first mandate makes no mention of

[1] *Cal. Papal Petitions*, I, p. 107.

difficulties, the second reveals opposition or a determination to exact heavy compensation which may well have been known or suspected from the beginning. For example, in 1330, Westminster Abbey obtained a papal bull commanding the bishop of Worcester to appropriate to it the church of Longdon in his diocese.[1] This he refused to do unless the abbot submitted to him his jurisdiction over Malvern Priory, and it was not until after a second mandate had been addressed to the bishop, in 1333,[2] that Westminster secured the church. Again, in 1352, Queen Philippa in a petition to the pope stated that at her request he had granted the appropriation of St Peter's, Northampton, to the hospital of St Katharine by the Tower of London, but that the master, brethren, and sisters had been unable "to obtain the execution of the appropriation from the bishop of Lincoln on the death of the last two rectors unless they paid a heavy pension, or bound themselves in a large sum of money", and she prayed that the bishop of London, the abbot of Westminster and the papal nuncio in England, might be ordered to make the appropriation.[3] Similarly, two papal mandates were required before Westminster Abbey could obtain the churches of Sawbridgeworth and Kelvedon,[4] and in the second of these it was said that the bishop of London, in whose diocese the churches were situated, neglected to obey the former mandate because his chapter and the archdeacons of Colchester and Middlesex opposed the appropriations. Further examples might easily be cited, and difficulties of the kind here described may be suspected whenever the pope granted that an appropriation might take effect without leave of the diocesan, or committed its execution to some person other than the bishop.

Occasionally, also, the papal authority was invoked to procure the restoration of a church which had been lost through the fault or misfortune of the appropriators. Thus the bull by which the church of Butleigh was appropriated to Glastonbury Abbey stated that the appropriation had been "defeated by the appointment to it by a former abbot of a clerk, who being instituted by the late bishop holds it to the loss of the monastery".[5]

[1] *Cal. Papal Letters*, II, p. 350. [2] *Ibid.* p. 393.
[3] *Cal. Papal Petitions*, I, pp. 236–7.
[4] *Cal. Papal Letters*, II, pp. 350, 394. [5] *Ibid.* p. 355.

But it is probable that the most frequent causes of recourse to Rome arose, directly or indirectly, out of the pope's interference with the ordinary rights of patronage. The pope exercised the right of providing to all benefices which had become void by the death or resignation of cardinals and papal chaplains, or by the death of any beneficed clerk who died at or within three days' journey of the Papal Court. Moreover, bishops and the heads of religious houses were constantly receiving mandates to present papal nominees to benefices in their gift. Such demands were not indeed confined to the benefices of ecclesiastical patrons, but in England they were usually withstood by the lay possessors of advowsons, while as a rule the ordinary rights of the ecclesiastical patron were entirely overruled by these claims of the papacy. If, then, a church was in the possession of a rector who had obtained it by papal authority, it was more than likely that on his death or resignation the vacancy would be filled by the same authority. Many of the churches for whose appropriation licences were obtained were at the time in the possession of persons who had procured them by the pope's assistance, and whose successors he was almost certain to appoint.

When a church was thus held, the would-be appropriators probably had little chance of success unless they induced the pope to make the appropriation and thereby prevented his appointing a successor to the then rector. Thus when, in 1333, Adam de Orleton obtained a bull appropriating the church of Blockley to the income of the bishops of Worcester, the church, although it had long been of the bishop's patronage, had for nearly forty years been held by a succession of papal officials, one of whom, John, bishop of Porto, was then in possession, and had Orleton not secured a papal grant of the appropriation, it is doubtful if he could ever have appropriated the church, or even, perhaps, have recovered the exercise of his rights of patronage. In this case of Blockley, the bishop seems to have encountered no opposition after the one papal grant had been procured, but other appropriations, even when papal licences had been granted, were less easily obtained. The Roman Court was not always consistent in upholding its original decisions, and the result was sometimes a protracted lawsuit which was discreditable to all concerned. The case of this kind, concerning which the fullest details have survived, relates to the appropriation to Newburgh Priory of the church of Owston in the diocese of Lincoln. In 1345, the prior and convent petitioned the pope for the appropriation of this church, and there is a suggestion of anticipated difficulty in their request that the vicar's portion should be taxed and assigned by the bishop of Carlisle, and in the pope's grant of their petition, on condition that compensation was made to the ordinary of the place according to the decision of the bishop of Carlisle or of Ely.[1] The fears which these measures seem to indicate were soon justified; for when, probably in 1348, Ralph de Gisburn, the rector, resigned, William de Navesby, the nephew of the bishop of Lincoln, endeavoured to obtain the church.[2] The story of the ensuing struggle, in which the monastery was eventually victorious, is best told in a petition which the prior and convent presented to the pope in 1352. In this they stated that

> the pope appropriated to them the church of Ouston,..., of their patronage, and that on its voidance by the resignation of Ralph de Gisburn they took possession of it. But afterwards William de Navesby, archdeacon of Chester, asserting that provision of the said church had been made to him by the bishop [of Lincoln], took and held it for some time, a suit being brought in the papal palace in which sentences were given in favour of the abbot[3] and convent. William, however, stating that Ralph's resignation having been made to the bishop, the pope, treating the church as void, and reserved before the said appropriation, gave it to William, who procured to be inducted, and has molested the said religious, who to avoid these grievances, and in fear of greater losses, made a money bargain with William, binding themselves by an oath, on which William renounced his pretended right to the said church, which is now held by the religious.[4]

In this case it seems clear that the interests of the bishop's kinsman would have effectually prevented the monastery from obtaining possession of Owston if the prior and convent had not secured the support of the pope, and although so determined a struggle was probably rare, similar difficulties must often have been feared.

Such reasons do not indeed account for all the papal appropriations, and no doubt many were obtained merely because,

[1] *Cal. Papal Petitions*, I, p. 86.
[2] *Cal. Papal Letters*, III, p. 347.
[3] *Sic*, in evident error for *prior*.
[4] *Cal. Papal Petitions*, I, pp. 227, 228.

since the pope was the highest authority, a grant made by him would be the most secure, but during most of the period under consideration, the papal assent was sought as a means of obtaining additional security or of overcoming particular difficulties, and not as a thing essential to the legality of an appropriation. This, in my opinion, was the position of the papacy with regard to appropriations until the year 1366. In that year Urban V published a decree annulling all appropriations that had not then taken effect, and forbidding the bishops to make appropriations for the next ten years. Similar decrees were issued by several of Urban's successors,[1] so that almost the same effect was produced as would have been created by a prohibition intended to last for all time. In view of Urban's general character as an opponent of ecclesiastical abuses, the honesty of his intentions to check by this means what was commonly regarded as a serious evil cannot be doubted. The decree certainly delayed many appropriations, but its success in lessening the number that were eventually appropriated may be questioned. For almost as soon as it had been published, the pope began to receive petitions to allow particular appropriations to be carried out, in spite of the general prohibition, and these petitions were seldom refused. But whatever may have been its effect on the number of appropriations, Urban's prohibition and the similar decrees which were issued by later popes brought about one important change, that whereas previous to 1366 an appropriation could legally be made by the diocesan without recourse to Rome, it was henceforth legal only if it was made with the pope's assent; for since the pope had decreed that no further appropriations were to take place, he alone could set aside this law. The ultimate effect of these prohibitions, then, was less to reduce the number of appropriations than to increase the papal control over this aspect of church life.

Consequently, the number of appropriations which according to the Calendars of Papal Letters and Petitions were granted or confirmed after 1366 is probably very nearly the actual number that were being appropriated. The number of English and Welsh appropriations which the last published volume of the Calendar of Papal Letters, 1455–1464, records is eleven, and the number that were licenced by the English Chancery during the same

[1] *Cal. Papal Letters*, IV, p. 180.

period is nine. The papal assent was usually sought after the royal licence had been obtained, and, therefore, the licences granted by the king and pope within a given period do not as a rule concern the same churches, but, since in the fifteenth century the rate of appropriations did not vary greatly, the figures thus obtained may be fairly compared. Here the papal grants and confirmations instead of amounting to about one-fourth of the royal licences, as was the case under Edward III, are slightly more numerous than the king's licences, but the difference is so slight that for practical purposes the numbers of papal and royal grants of appropriations may be regarded as approximately equal.

The number of churches, then, which according to the Papal Letters were being appropriated in the middle of the fifteenth century is, approximately, the actual number, while the numbers which the same source gives for the periods immediately before and after the Black Death represent only an uncertain proportion of those that were then being appropriated: the actual numbers being somewhere between the numbers of royal and papal licences, but probably much nearer to the former. When the statistics compiled from the royal licences are examined[1] as evidence of the effect on appropriations of the Black Death, it appears that during the years immediately following the pestilence, licences continued to be issued at approximately the same rate as before, but that, soon after, the numbers fell far below those of Edward III's early years.

The statistics based on the royal licences, therefore, considerably strengthen the conclusions already put forward by Dr Coulton that the Black Death did not increase the number of appropriations.[2] The diminution in the number of licences which appears soon after the pestilence may, as has been suggested, be due in part to the fact that the parishes as well as the monasteries had been impoverished, but it seems to have been mainly owing to other causes. Of these causes, the altered relations of the papacy towards appropriations after 1366 was probably one. It is noteworthy that the annual number of licences issued had begun to fall well before 1366, but the decrees of Urban and his successors, by indirectly imposing the necessity of seeking papal

[1] See table at the end of this chapter.

[2] *History Teachers' Miscellany*, IV, No. 3, p. 38.

approval, may have deterred many who might otherwise have granted churches to monasteries and chantries, and thus have kept the numbers of appropriations from again rising. But the main causes of the change were probably the comparatively small number of new foundations, and the fact that for such as were established the revenues of suppressed alien priories provided a large proportion of the endowments.

From this we may go on to examine a subject on which the Patent Rolls are even more instructive—the layman's interest in appropriations. The theory has been advanced that, in the eleventh and twelfth centuries, the lay lords who owned advowsons took from the parishes as much as the monastic or other appropriators, and it has been further suggested that lay tithe-holders continued to be numerous all through the Middle Ages. The principal argument which was employed in support of this view was the tenacity with which the lay lords clung to their right of patronage. How far this theory may be true of the eleventh and twelfth centuries I am not in a position to discuss, but I have found no trace of lay tithe-holders in the fourteenth century and, moreover, the evidence contained in the Patent Rolls shows that there were other reasons sufficient to induce the average lay lord to offer opposition to any interference with his rights of patronage. For though the lord might not be able to take the proceeds from the parishes, he might, and very often did, dispose of them in a way that was decidedly to his financial advantage.

It must be remembered that owing to the religious beliefs of the time, provision for the future welfare of his soul was an important matter to the average medieval man, and that this provision largely took the form of conventional works of piety, such as gifts to monasteries or the founding of chantries. But to grant lands for such purposes reduced the income of the grantor and his heirs, while to grant an advowson and obtain a licence for the appropriation of the church would give all the spiritual advantages which might be obtained by a grant of land without involving a corresponding diminution of the goods of this world. The possibility of this motive is suggested by the number of licences obtained for the appropriation of churches to new foundations. Licences were issued for the appropriation of eight churches to the priory of Maxstock, which William de Clinton, the earl of Huntingdon, founded early in the reign of Edward III; the chantry which John de Poultney, a rich citizen of London, founded in the church of St Laurence, Candlewick Street, was to have the revenues of seven churches; five churches were appropriated to Edington Priory; while the king's new foundations of St Stephen's, Westminster, and St George's, Windsor, were given licences to appropriate five and eleven churches respectively. That the endowments of any ecclesiastical organization should consist in part of appropriated churches was a great advantage, since the income derived from churches was termed spiritualities and could not therefore be seized into the king's hands. This is brought out clearly in a petition, concerning the appropriation of the church of Bishopsteignton to the see of Exeter, which John de Grandisson addressed to the pope in 1329, and in which he gave as the principal reason for the appropriation that the income of the see consisted mainly of temporalities which came into the king's hands in times of voidance of the bishopric and often at other times.[1] Such considerations may well have been in the minds of some of those who were responsible for the appropriation of churches, but there is evidence pointing to the conclusion that economy might also be the motive. In 1351, John de Insula of Rougemont, who was founding a chantry by endowing the monastery of Bolton in Craven in order that they might find chaplains to celebrate divine service for him and his ancestors, obtained a licence to grant for this purpose the advowson of the church of Harwood, and for the monastery to appropriate the church,[2] but about a year later he procured other letters patent enabling him to grant to the abbot and convent of Bolton land and rent out of his manor of Harwood to the yearly value of forty pounds "until he shall obtain for them the appropriation of the church of Harwood".[3]

The king, as might have been expected, made free use of his power of granting licences for appropriations to increase the number of masses said for his soul and to further works of piety in which he was interested. The most interesting of these, to a modern student, is the grant made in his thirty-seventh year to

[1] *Reg. John de Grandisson*, ed. Hingeston-Randolph, I, pp. 103, 104.
[2] *Cal. Pat. Rolls*, 1350–54, p. 177. [3] *Ibid.* 1350–54, p. 352.

the abbot and convent of St Mary de Pratis, Leicester, of a licence to appropriate the church of Kirkby Mallory. Out of its revenues the monastery was to maintain two canons at the university, one of whom should be bound to say mass daily for the king's good estate, except in the vacations of the university.[1]

In addition to supporting works of piety, the king, at least occasionally, used the grant of church revenues as a means of adding to his temporal possessions or of recovering those that his ancestors had alienated. This is shown in the records concerning the appropriation to the prior and convent of Leeds, in Kent, of the church of Leatherhead in the diocese of Winchester. The letters touching this matter, which the king, at the request of Queen Isabella, sent to the pope, mention only the losses sustained by the convent when Leeds Castle was besieged during the late reign and the need of rebuilding the church;[2] but letters patent state that the canons maintained a chantry in the castle chapel for the soul of Queen Eleanor, and that, to support the chantry, Edward I had granted to the monastery twenty-eight marks yearly out of his manor of Leeds until he or his heirs should provide them with land, rent, or ecclesiastical benefices to that value, and that because Edward III was granting the church of Leatherhead to the prior and convent, they agreed to add two canons to those celebrating in the castle and released their claim to the twenty-eight marks.[3]

Another instance of the same thing is a grant to Notley Priory of the advowson of the church of Lillingstone, with licence to appropriate the church, in return for which the convent released their right to an annual supply of firewood granted to them by King John.[4] After three years, during which the convent had not been able to appropriate the church because it had not been vacant, on their petition to the king showing that they had neither the church nor the firewood, they were granted for three years a pension of twelve and a half marks at the Exchequer, on condition that it should cease as soon as they appropriated the church, and that they used all diligence in obtaining the appropriation.[5]

In some other cases, the grant of an advowson with a licence

[1] *Cal. Pat. Rolls*, 1361–64, p. 413.
[2] *Cal. Papal Petitions*, I, p. 85.
[3] *Cal. Pat. Rolls*, 1340–43, p. 333.
[4] *Ibid.* 1354–58, p. 20.
[5] *Ibid.* 1354–58, p. 540.

to appropriate the church seems to have been adopted as a means of saving other expenditure. Thus in August 1339, Edward III gave to the abbot and convent of St Michael, Antwerp, the advowson of the valuable church of Finedon, then taxed at forty pounds, and a licence to appropriate this church. The letters patent state that "This grant is made in consideration of the long stay which the king and queen Philippa have made in the abbey and of the great easements which they have had there, as well as of the fact that the king's son Lionel has been born there and baptized in the church of the abbey".[1] This was followed, in December of that year, by a request from the king, addressed to the bishop of Lincoln, the subdean and chapter and others interested, to do quickly what is requisite for the appropriation of Finedon to the abbot and convent of the monastery of St Michael, Antwerp, to whom the king has granted the advowson in return for their hospitality to the queen.[2]

Another way by which the grant of advowsons with licences to appropriate the churches might be turned to the king's profit is illustrated by an item in the Patent Rolls of 1326. It shows that Walter Langton, late bishop of Coventry and Lichfield, had purposed to assign the manor of Greenford, co. Middlesex, to the church of Lichfield to find and maintain chantries and alms for the souls of the late king and others, but that, instead, he had granted the manor to the king, who, in return, gave him the advowsons of the churches of Chesterton, co. Warwick, and Worfield, in Shropshire, and granted licence for him to assign the advowsons to any ecclesiastical persons, religious or others, in his diocese, and for such persons to appropriate the churches.[3]

In addition to the instances already cited, a few grants of appropriations for unusual purposes may be briefly mentioned. In 1330, the abbot and convent of Bury St Edmunds were granted licence to appropriate the churches of Rougham and Thurston "in consideration of the grievous losses sustained by them at the hands of the men of Bury St Edmunds, and because, at the king's request, they have pardoned a great part of the sum recovered by them as damages".[4] Another remarkable licence which was issued in 1354 to enable the abbot and convent

[1] *Cal. Pat. Rolls*, 1338–40, p. 313.
[2] *Ibid.* 1338–40, p. 404.
[3] *Ibid.* 1324–27, p. 252.
[4] *Ibid.* 1327–30, 546.

of St Mary, York, to appropriate the church of Rudston, states that this was granted to pacify dissensions which had lately arisen between the abbot and convent, and the mayor and citizens of the city,[1] but unfortunately there seems no means of discovering what had caused these dissensions, or how the appropriation of Rudston was expected to appease them. But perhaps the most interesting of all the licences which the Patent Rolls of this period contain is one which was issued, in 1361, for the alienation in mortmain by John Bardolf of Wyrmegeye, to the prior and convent of the house of Shouldham and the nuns there, of the advowson of the church of Holy Trinity, Caistor, and for them to appropriate the church, "in aid of the sustenance of Margaret de Monte Forti, daughter of Thomas de Bello Campo, earl of Warwick, Katharine daughter of Guy de Warrewyk, deceased (*defuncti*), and Elizabeth sister of the said John, nuns of the house".[2]

Arrangements such as these show that the appropriation of parish churches might be as much to the interest of the lay lord as of the ecclesiastical organization to which their revenues were assigned. How the parishes whose tithes were thus disposed of were affected is a matter about which few persons of that age seem to have cared.

The purely mercenary attitude with which church revenues were sometimes regarded is well illustrated by a commission of Oyer and Terminer of the year 1319, which was issued on the complaint of Philip de Buckton, parson of the church of Weston. This document recites his accusations against a number of persons mentioned by name who, he alleged,

> by night entered his church and dwelling-place and also his manor at Weston, co. Northampton, broke and burned the doors and windows of his said dwelling-place, manor and church, and took and carried away books, vestments and ornaments of his said church, and also his goods and certain charters and muniments of his, and assaulted Simon le Carter, his servant, in the said church, so that by the violent effusion of blood therein, the said church remained for a long time under interdict, whereby he lost the profits of his church and the service of his servant....[3]

In this case, we must observe that it was not an appropriating

[1] *Cal. Pat. Rolls*, 1354–58, p. 4.
[2] *Ibid.* 1361–64, p. 111.
[3] *Ibid.* 1317–21, p. 472.

body, but an ordinary rector, who complained that he had lost the profits of his church. And indifference to the welfare of the parishes was as marked in the presentations to rectories as in the appropriations of churches; for the lords profited most by their possession of advowsons in being able to present their relations and the clerks in their service, and thereby saving the payment of pensions or salaries which would otherwise have been necessary. As a result of this system many of the richest benefices were held by papal officials and king's clerks who were habitually non-resident. Moreover, the rectors of many other churches were presented when they were in minor orders and immediately given leave to attend schools or universities. Such conditions might, of course, be only temporary evils, but in many parishes they must have existed so regularly as to seem, to contemporaries, permanent.

Before, therefore, the appropriators are too severely condemned for their readiness to convert to their own uses tithes which might better have been spent in the parishes by which they were paid, some attempt should be made to ascertain how these tithes had been spent before they came into the hands of the monasteries or other appropriating bodies. The ideal method of answering this question would be to study the careers of the rectors of each church during the forty or fifty years immediately preceding its appropriation; but the number of churches is too great and information concerning their rectors too difficult to obtain for this to be practicable. I have, therefore, found it necessary to make a selection of the churches to be considered in this way. It seemed fairest to choose a number of churches in different parts of the country which were appropriated at different times, and as a safeguard against the temptation of choosing particularly interesting churches I have taken the seventy-five for the appropriation of which papal authority was obtained between 1330 and 1348. This group includes churches of every diocese in England; and their values, according to the Taxation of Pope Nicholas, vary from seven marks to seventy. I think, therefore, that the results obtained by an examination of how these churches had been served may be regarded as a fair indication of the results that would be obtained by the more laborious study of a larger number of churches.

In trying to discover what class of men had been the rectors of these churches I have consulted the printed episcopal registers, and from them have obtained a number of useful items; but I have found more valuable the papal provisions and dispensations to pluralists given in the Calendar of Papal Letters and the protections and presentations to livings in the king's gift in the Calendar of Patent Rolls. Even when all these sources have been searched, there remain many churches about the rectors of which so little is known that it is impossible to judge what effect their appropriation had on the parishes; and in only a few cases can a really satisfactory list of incumbents be compiled.

One of the churches concerning which we have the fullest information is Blockley in the diocese of Worcester, a rich benefice which was taxed at thirty-seven pounds. It was in the gift of the bishop of Worcester, but, in 1294, he had presented to it one Peter de Escot,[1] who had obtained holy orders by concealing the fact of his illegitimacy, and who, as soon as he became rector of Blockley, set out for the Roman Court, apparently to seek a dispensation.[2] While there, he died, and the pope, availing himself of his right to present to the benefices of those who died at the Apostolic See, gave Blockley to Bartholomew de Ferentino, chamberlain of Benedict, cardinal of SS. Cosmas and Damian.[3] Who was Bartholomew's immediate successor is not stated, but an item in the Calendar of Patent Rolls relating to a chantry at Blockley shows that in 1314 the church was held by Benedict de Paston,[4] whom we know, from other sources, to have been a papal chaplain. In September 1330, the rectory, void by his death, was conferred on Master Gerald de Pristinio,[5] and in 1332, when Gerald became bishop of Agde, Blockley was granted in commendam to John, bishop of Porto.[6] He seems to have been its last rector; for the next year Adam de Orleton obtained a papal licence to appropriate it to the income of the bishops of Worcester "to take effect on the death or resignation of the bishop of Porto".[7]

Another church whose list of rectors is unusually complete is

[1] *Reg. Godfrey Giffard*, ed. J. W. Willis-Bund, II, p. 447.
[2] *Ibid.* II, p. 451.
[3] *Cal. Papal Letters*, I, p. 559.
[4] *Cal. Pat. Rolls*, 1313–17, p. 159.
[5] *Cal. Papal Letters*, II, p. 337.
[6] *Ibid.* II, p. 370.
[7] *Ibid.* II, p. 382.

Brough under Stainmoor, in the diocese of Carlisle. In 1291, a papal dispensation allowed John de Langton to hold it, together with another church, provided that a fitting portion of the fruits was spent on the churches.[1] In 1299, while Langton was the king's chancellor and still only in subdeacon's orders, he received, at the king's request, a dispensation to hold the treasurership of Wells, eight prebends (named), and seven churches, of which Brough under Stainmoor was one, and to accept two other benefices if canonically offered him.[2] In 1305, when John became bishop of Chichester, Hugh de Burgh, another king's clerk, was presented.[3] He held it until 1323, when it was given to William de Norwich,[4] and its next and last rector was Robert de Eglesfield,[5] presented in 1332, during whose tenure of the church licences were obtained for its appropriation to Queen's College, Oxford.[6]

Brough under Stainmoor was of the king's patronage and was therefore particularly liable to be held by his clerks, but churches in the gift of monasteries or bishops were often no more fortunate, as the king presented to these when the temporalities were in his hands, and at other times their patrons frequently made presentations in accordance with the king's wishes. Moreover, churches of ecclesiastical patronage were always likely to be secured by those who obtained papal provisions or reservations. Thus, Sawbridgeworth, in the gift of Westminster Abbey, was held by a succession of king's clerks, of whom the most famous was Richard de Bury, the future bishop of Durham.[7]

Altogether, out of the seventy-five churches considered here, I find twenty-five which, during the half century preceding the issue of the licences for their appropriation, had been held at least twice by king's clerks, papal officers, or others who would not reside.

For the purpose of comparison I have made a similar examination of the rectors of twenty-five churches, for the appropriation of which royal licences were issued during the last twelve years

[1] *Cal. Papal Letters*, I, p. 526.
[2] *Ibid.* I, p. 581.
[3] *Cal. Pat. Rolls*, 1301–07, p. 375.
[4] *Ibid.* 1321–24, p. 326.
[5] *Ibid.* 1330–34, p. 251.
[6] *Ibid.* 1340–43, p. 249; *Cal. Papal Letters*, III, p. 88.
[7] *Reg. Stephen Gravesend*, ed. R. C. Fowler (Cant. and York Soc.), VII, p. 287.

of the reign of Edward III, and in this group I have found seven held by rectors who must have been unsatisfactory.

There is too little evidence to show how the other churches in these groups were served; but, though the absence of references to them in the Papal Letters and Patent Rolls may imply that they were held by men who were neither royal nor papal officers, it is no proof that they were well served; and as in several instances where I have been able to discover the name of only one rector, he has been a clerk of the king or of some great lord, and unlikely, owing to his other occupations, to assume much personal responsibility for the welfare of his parish,[1] I believe that if more complete information were available the number of churches having unsatisfactory rectors would be considerably higher.

In the case of churches, such as I have discussed above, which must have been accustomed to non-resident rectors, the appropriation probably did little or no immediate harm, and indeed the substitution, for a hired chaplain removable at the rector's pleasure, of a perpetual vicar with a fixed stipend apportioned by the bishop would seem a more satisfactory arrangement, both for the parishes and for their priests.

In these circumstances, some of those who promoted appropriations may well have felt that in so doing they were really serving the interests of religion. That this was the view of one fourteenth-century ecclesiastic is shown by the opening sentences of a petition which Richard de Bury addressed to the pope in 1342. He begins by stating

that in his diocese there is a fat (*pinguis*) parish church called Hoghton, which, when void, has been collated by bishops of Durham at the instance of kings and queens of England, to courtiers, insufficient and light persons who turn the income to lascivious and profane uses, and since, when it becomes void, the said Richard will have to do the same, he desires that the income shall be spent on the increase of divine worship and the good of the state in those parts, which need lettered men.[2]

The extent to which any appropriation actually enriched the

[1] In 1300, Swaneton was held by Robert de Vanna, chaplain of Leonard, bishop of Albano, *Cal. Papal Letters*, I, p. 588; in 1331, John de Tiddeswell, a king's clerk, was rector of Hermeston, *Cal. Pat. Rolls*, 1330–34, p. 118; in 1355, the church of Leeke, Lincolnshire, was held by Walter Power, then a clerk of Henry, duke of Lancaster, *Cal. Papal Petitions*, I, p. 271.

[2] *Cal. Papal Petitions*, I, p. 25.

house that obtained it is difficult to estimate. Gascoigne, writing in the middle of the fifteenth century, stated that benefices rapidly diminished in value when they had been appropriated, and accused the monks of seeking fresh appropriations as soon as the income from the churches which they already held began to decrease.[1] But whether or not the appropriated church would eventually diminish in value, it would not at once become a source of profit. For no appropriation could be obtained without expense. Unfortunately, it is impossible to discover precisely how much was spent in any single case, and the amount doubtless varied greatly according to the circumstances under which the appropriation was made, but there is plenty of evidence as to the various kinds of payments that might be required to show that the cost cannot have been light.

From the Peterhouse bursar's roll of 1396–97,[2] we learn that at that time the college spent £10. 15*s*. 6½*d*. on business connected with the appropriation of the church of Cherryhinton. The items which make up this total are the lawyers' fees, and the incidental expenses of prosecuting a suit against the bishop of Ely, in the Court of Arches. As, according to the Taxation of Pope Nicholas IV, the church was valued at thirty pounds, the amount thus spent is small in comparison with what would be gained if the appropriation could be secured, but there is nothing to indicate that the expenses would have been less had the church been of smaller value, and, moreover, the suit in the Court of Arches is only one of the expenses which this appropriation involved. In May 1345, five pounds had been paid for a royal licence allowing Simon, then bishop of Ely, to grant the advowson of the church to Peterhouse, and the warden and scholars to appropriate the church.[3] Eight years later, this licence was renewed, because Simon had died before the original licence had taken effect[4] and, about the same time, the pope's assent to the appropriation was sought and obtained. We do not know the cost of obtaining the renewal of the royal licence or of the visit to the Apostolic See, but both must have involved considerable expense.

Fuller details are available concerning the appropriation to

[1] *Loci e Libro Veritatum*, p. 115.

[2] I owe my knowledge of this item to the kindness of Mr L. F. Salzman.

[3] *Cal. Pat. Rolls*, 1343–45, p. 460.

[4] *Ibid.* 1350–54, pp. 493–4.

Merton College, Oxford, of the church of Embleton in the diocese of Durham, which took place early in Edward III's reign. The bursar's accounts for the year 1331 contain itemized accounts of the expenses of two journeys;[1] one to the Papal Court at Avignon, and the other to the court of the bishop of Durham. The accounts include the fees paid on each occasion and probably, therefore, represent the sum of the expenses incurred in obtaining the assent of the ecclesiastical authorities. When the items here given are added, we find that they reach a total of £48. 6*s*. 0½*d*. But the appropriation cost the college more than is here specified, for we learn from an item on the patent roll of 1328, that the warden and scholars paid ten marks for a pardon of their trespass in having acquired the advowson of Embleton from Edmund, late earl of Lancaster, without a royal licence,[2] and, to obtain this pardon and a licence to appropriate,[3] a number of minor expenses, of which there is no record, must have been required. Altogether, then, the college spent at least £54. 19*s*. 4½*d*. on securing this appropriation. Whether this outlay was justified by the profits which the college might reasonably hope that Embleton would yield, there is no means of judging. The value of the benefice is mentioned in none of the documents relating to the appropriation, and in the Taxation of Pope Nicholas, it appears in a list of churches which are described as "vastuta et penitus destructa",[4] but from the fact that a succession of important king's clerks appear to have thought it worth their while to hold the rectory, we may infer that its poverty had been greatly exaggerated. Nevertheless, the profits are unlikely to have been large, and it may therefore safely be assumed that several years would have to elapse before Embleton could be regarded as a source of revenue to the college.

In the Merton accounts just cited, one of the largest items was a sum of £13. 6*s*. 8*d*., described as "eleemosine Epi Dunelm", which was probably the payment by which the bishop was recompensed for the loss which he would sustain through the appropriation. Both the Patent Rolls and the Papal Letters

[1] Printed in Thorold Rogers' *History of Agriculture and Prices in England*, II, pp. 631–41.
[2] *Cal. Pat. Rolls*, 1327–30, p. 260.
[3] *Ibid*. 1327–30, p. 490.
[4] *Taxatio Ecclesiastica P. Nicholai*, p. 331 (52).

frequently mention the compensation which bishops received when churches in their dioceses were appropriated; the grant of a small annual pension, amounting very often to one mark, being the commonest form of this compensation. Such a charge was not in itself heavy, but it would, of course, somewhat reduce the profits of the newly acquired church.

But except perhaps when an appropriation seemed likely to affect the interests of the papacy, the heaviest item of expense was probably the fine exacted for the royal licence. A fine was indeed not invariably required. Licences for appropriations that were really to the king's advantage were, as might be expected, issued without the payment of a fine, and from time to time persons high in the royal favour obtained licences for which nothing was charged. Thus when, in 1335, letters patent allowing the appropriation of Blockley to the see of Worcester were issued, they were described as having been granted "in recognition of the constancy of the faith and love towards the king and the various labours in his service of William de Monte Acuto, the bishop's kinsman, as well as for the special affection which the king bears to the bishop".[1] But as a rule a fine was charged, and its amount was often very considerable. Sometimes, instead of actually paying fines, the monasteries obtained the king's assent to their appropriations by agreeing that some debt which the king owed them should be cancelled. In 1343, for example, the monastery of Abingdon obtained a licence to appropriate the church of Uffington, which was valued at £39. 18*s*. 0*d*.,[2] "at the request of the king's kinswoman, the countess of Ulster, and because the abbot and convent have released to the king 100 marks wherein he was bound to them by letters patent which they have surrendered".[3] This sum, when the value of the church is taken into account, appears small in comparison with the sum which ten years later the abbot and convent of Revesby gave to obtain the church of Theddlethorpe. For the licence by which they were allowed to acquire the advowson in mortmain and to appropriate the church was granted "in consideration of the surrender by the abbot of Revesby of letters patent whereby the king was held to him in 115*l*. for

[1] *Cal. Pat. Rolls*, 1334–38, p. 120. [2] *Taxatio Ecclesiastica P. Nicholai*, p. 62.
[3] *Cal. Pat. Rolls*, 1343–45, p. 51.

wool lent to him by the abbot".[1] The value of the church as stated in this licence was ten marks, but the Taxation of Pope Nicholas gives it as eight pounds.[2] Even this higher figure is probably an underestimate of the church's value, but since the abbey would be required to maintain a vicar it is likely that the actual profits would not much exceed eight pounds. If this was so, more than fourteen years would have to pass before Theddlethorpe had yielded a sum equivalent to the amount of the cancelled debt. Moreover, in Richard II's reign, before the church was actually appropriated, a further sum of £40 was paid as a fine for a renewal of the licence.[3] The expenses sustained by Revesby were certainly extraordinary, but there are many examples of heavy fines.

When all the expenses that might arise from an attempt to appropriate a church are considered, it is not surprising to find that the master and scholars of Michaelhouse did not appropriate the church of Cheadle of which they were the patrons, because the cost would be too great, or that Bishop Roger Norbury, when visiting the monastery of Roucester in Dovedale, should find it burdened with a heavy debt incurred "in curia et extra" in trying to get the appropriation of the church of Woodford in the diocese of Lincoln.[4] In fact, though the heavy expenses involved in obtaining an appropriation seem rarely to have deterred a religious house from seeking this form of endowment, and were seldom so frankly admitted as a cause of poverty as at the Roucester visitation, they must often have been severely felt. No doubt a church would usually become in the end a profitable possession, but, in many cases, an appropriation must have been a most unsatisfactory means of seeking relief from a pressing financial burden.

Finally, something should be said with regard to the alleged greed of the monasteries as shown in their haste to obtain possession of their churches when once the licences to appropriate had been granted. It was almost invariably contained in both the ecclesiastical and the royal licence, that the appropriation should take effect on the death or resignation of the then rector. This

[1] *Cal. Pat. Rolls*, 1350–54, p. 479. [2] *Taxatio Ecclesiastica P. Nicholai*, p. 59.
[3] *Cal. Pat. Rolls*, 1391–96, p. 579.
[4] *Register of Roger de Norbury* (William Salt Archaeol. Soc.), I, p. 266.

provision was doubtless necessary for the protection of the incumbent's interests, but to the appropriators it was often the indirect cause of many difficulties which might prevent them from obtaining possession of a church long after it had ceased to be occupied by the rector on whose behalf the stipulation had originally been made. For while the rule that the appropriation could not be carried out until the death or resignation of the rector was strictly enforced, the would-be appropriators had no positive assurance that the church would be given to them on its next voidance. Their chances of securing it would depend on the circumstances in which the vacancy occurred. If the church became void at a time when the temporalities of the monastery or other appropriator were in the king's hands, he was likely to exercise his customary right of presenting to the rectory. Thus, shortly after the licence for the appropriation of the church of Longdon to the abbot and convent of Westminster had been issued, the church became vacant while the abbey was in the king's hands on account of the death of the last abbot, and immediately he presented a king's clerk to be rector of Longdon.[1] In this case, the king had a genuine interest in the appropriation since it had been granted to compensate the monastery for the losses it had sustained from a serious fire which had broken out in the adjacent palace of Westminster,[2] and it was probably owing to this consideration that the king revoked his presentation, about two months after it had been made.[3] But the letter in which this was made known, by stating that "the king has thought fit to revoke the presentation", implies that he was granting a favour rather than acknowledging the monastery's right. If such was the view held by the king and his lawyers, it would be difficult, if not impossible, for a monastery under similar circumstances to induce the king to revoke a presentation unless he had some special reason for wishing the appropriation to proceed without delay.

Difficulties were also likely to arise if the rector died at the Apostolic See, or if he obtained promotion in any way which would give the pope a claim to provide a successor to his benefice. In such cases, though the appropriators would prob-

[1] *Cal. Pat. Rolls*, 1330–34, p. 543. [2] *Cal. Papal Letters*, II, p. 350.
[3] *Cal. Pat. Rolls*, 1330–34, p. 569.

ably obtain the church in the end, a suit at the Papal Court, which might be both long and costly, would in most instances be necessary before their claims were established.

In other ways, also, the delay which resulted from the necessity of waiting until the next voidance placed serious obstacles in the way of the appropriators. The rector might retain the church for many years after the licence to appropriate had been granted, and, meanwhile, changes disadvantageous to the appropriators might take place. A bishop who was known to favour an appropriation might be succeeded by one who would use all his power to prevent it, and whose opposition could be overcome only by recourse to Rome. Such a case may be illustrated from the Papal Letters concerning the appropriation to Merton College of the church of Ponteland in the diocese of Durham. The petition of the warden, scholars and brethren of the college stated that

> When Peter de Montfort, patron of Ponteland, with consent of the bishop, gave that church to the said house, bishop R., with consent of his chapter, appropriated it to them, to take effect on the death or resignation of the rector and two portionaries, by whom the church was served. One of the portionaries resigned, the other died, and thereupon the warden, scholars, and brethren of the house entered into possession of the portions; but on the death of the rector, bishop A.,[1] thirsting to obtain the collation, the church being worth 200 marks a year, sent armed men, who turned out the scholars they found there, and gave the rectory to Adam de Driffield, and the portions to Philip de Wileby and Charles de Bellomonte.[2]

The accession of a new king was also to be feared as an obstacle to appropriations, for this would necessitate the obtaining of a new licence, or a confirmation of the one already issued, and though it was not likely to be refused, it could not be procured without some delay and expense. That the new king's assent was required is suggested by a number of renewed licences and confirmations which were issued under Richard II, and the law on the point is clearly set forth in the following pardon which, in 1397, was granted to the prior and convent of Shouldham.

> Whereas by licence of the late king John Bardolf of Wyrmegeye granted the advowson of Holy Trinity, Castre, co. Norfolk, held in

[1] The bishops referred to were Robert of Holy Island and Anthony Bek.
[2] *Cal. Papal Letters*, I, pp. 605, 606.

chief, to the prior and convent of Shouldham, who had the licence to appropriate the same in mortmain, pending which suit during the late reign the church became void by the resignation of Simon Noreys, chaplain, whereupon the prior and convent presented William Walcote, and on his resignation John Mayhewe of Oxwyk, chaplain, who was accordingly admitted, instituted and inducted; subsequently licence to appropriate and appoint a vicar being obtained from the Pope, in the fourteenth year of the king's reign and the church being void by the death of the said John Mayhewe, the prior and convent, understanding that the late king's said licence would be sufficient without the king's licence or confirmation, appropriated the church and appointed William Barton vicar, assigning him his portion, with the assent of the ordinary, and have thus held possession of the same: the king, on their petition, pardons both their predecessors the trespasses by them committed herein and themselves their trespasses and the forfeiture incurred, and ratifies and confirms their estate in the church and rectory and William Barton's estate in the vicarage, notwithstanding any presentations to either heretofore made or any suit pending in the court.[1]

To what extent obstacles such as we have been considering actually prevented appropriations, it is impossible to say, but it is certain that in many cases, when both royal and papal assent had been obtained, the licences remained unexecuted, and the failure to secure at least some of the churches which they concern may fairly be attributed to difficulties of the kind here described. This may go far to explain the seemingly undue haste with which the monasteries, when once a licence for the appropriation of a church had been obtained, endeavoured to cause it to be executed. As has been said above, both ecclesiastical and secular law required that the appropriation should take effect on the death or resignation of the existing rector, and the fear that, if matters were allowed to take their course, the voidance might occur at a time when the appropriators would be unable to take advantage of it, must often have led them to try to arrange for the rectories to become void at an opportune time for themselves. Various methods were adopted to induce the rector to resign at an early date. Through a monastery's own patronage, or by the help of some official in church or state, the parson might be presented to a benefice of equal or greater value which would necessitate his resigning the church. When this could not be

[1] *Cal. Pat. Rolls*, 1396–99, p. 253.

done, an agreement to pay the rector a pension might induce him to resign. Such a transaction savoured of simony, and it is probably for that reason that detailed accounts of these bargains are comparatively rare. In a few cases, however, the exact amount which the rector was to receive has been recorded. One which may be quoted as an example received royal confirmation, and has thus been preserved on the Patent Rolls.

Whereas the king lately recovered his presentation to the church of Beckeford which the abbot and convent of the monastery of St Mary in Cormeilles in Normandy, previously held appropriated as annexed to their cell of Newent, and presented thereto one Thomas Hervy, and whereas afterwards, taking into consideration the estate and possession which the abbot and convent had long had in the church and the form and cause of the recovery, he granted to them in mortmain the advowson of the said church; and whereas the said Thomas now purposes to resign the church to secure that the abbot and convent may not after his decease be impeached in any wise over his entry into the same, whereupon the abbot and convent, out of gratitude, have made petition to the king for licence to assign to the said Thomas a rent of 40*l.* for life out of their manor of Newent, co. Gloucester, now in the king's hand on account of the war with France, with power of distraint; the king has granted to them the licence prayed for.[1]

While such a pension was being paid the monastery can have derived but small profit from the church, and had it been certain that churches could be appropriated at any time after the necessary licences had been obtained, it is unlikely that the monasteries would have made such determined efforts to remove the rectors. These efforts show, in my opinion, not so much that the appropriators were unduly impatient to secure their possessions, but that they feared the difficulties in which delay might involve them.

Whether, when all the necessary consents had been obtained, any formal act was necessary to complete an appropriation is a matter which no modern authority on this subject has discussed, and indeed it is a matter concerning which our medieval records are seldom instructive. Among the documents belonging to the dean and chapter of Wells, however, there is one which gives a very full account of the ceremony by which in 1396 the dean and

[1] *Cal. Pat. Rolls*, 1370–74, p. 254.

chapter entered into possession of the church of Pucklechurch in the diocese of Worcester. To what extent the ceremony described in this record may be regarded as typical it is, of course, impossible to say, but since, in that age, most transactions were witnessed by some formal act, it is very probable that a similar ceremony was usually observed. The document, therefore, seems of sufficient interest to merit quoting at length. It is a

Declaration by Nicholas More clerk of the diocese of Wells, notary public, that on 12 November 1396 in his presence, Master Richard Harewell and Master Richard Bruton canons of Wells, professing themselves to be proctors of the dean and chapter, being in the porch of the church of Pokulchirche, the said Master Richard Bruton, by authority of a bull of Pope Boniface IX touching the appropriation of the said church to the said dean and chapter, and of letters under the great seal of King Richard (both of which he inspected), opened the door of the said church, and entered therein, with Richard Harewell the said notary and the witnesses, and advancing to the high altar took possession of the church in the name of the dean and chapter, and in sign thereof took in their hands the books, missals, chalices and ornaments of the church, rang or caused to be rung the church bells, and remaining in the chancel while high mass was celebrated caused the said papal and royal letters to be published, and their effect to be declared before a great concourse of people in the vulgar tongue, and on the same day entered and took possession of the rectory manse: and after on the 13 November held a court of the church tenants in the hall of the said rectory, who appeared before the said proctors and acknowledging the said dean and chapter for their lords, gave their oaths of fealty.[1]

In what I have said it has not been my intention to minimize the evils resulting from appropriations. No one, I think, who remembers how the system was opposed by some of the best of medieval ecclesiastics, and sees the lasting harm to the parishes for which it was responsible, can seriously defend it; but I have tried to show that, in many cases, the evils resulting from appropriations may have been less apparent to contemporaries than they are to us, and that the system was encouraged and to some extent excused by the selfish attitude with which the possession of an advowson was habitually regarded.

[1] *Calendar of the Manuscripts of the Dean and Chapter of Wells*, I, pp. 357–8.

Royal Licences for appropriation of Churches issued under Edward III

Regnal year	Number of licences	Regnal year	Number of licences
1	11	26	17
2	17	27	12
3	12	28	15
4	18	29	10
5	12	30	5 (165)
6	16	31	4
7	9	32	4
8	14	33	6
9	11	34	5
10	11 (131)	35	11
11	13	36	7
12	16	37	11
13	4	38	4
14	18	39	6
15	12	40	3 (61)
16	22	41	2
17	11	42	1
18	16	43	2
19	18	44	—
20	26 (156)	45	2
21	12	46	1
22	28	47	4
23	14	48	3
24	14	49	1
25	38	50	6
		51	4 (26)
			539

CHAPTER VI

CONCLUSION

DIVERSE as are the subjects with which the foregoing chapters have been concerned, there are three problems of general interest, towards an understanding of which they all contribute. These are the position of the church in public opinion; the effects of the Black Death; and the relations of the church to the central government, and in the present chapter I propose to discuss very briefly the evidence relating to these three subjects.

(1) *The Position of the Church in Public Opinion*

As a rule, students have sought for expressions of public opinion mainly in contemporary chronicles, poems and letters, and in such official records as the petitions presented in parliament. But public opinion may also be estimated from other records which at first appear less promising, and such are the documents with which we have been dealing. They contain very few definite statements of opinion, but they are of great value in bringing before us a multitude of men and women, of all classes, in one of the few relations with the church in which the individual was free to express his own wishes and tastes, that of benefactors, whose actions often tell us quite as much as any definite statement of their views, with regard to what they were thinking of the church and churchmen of their own day. Moreover, some of the documents we have been considering contain valuable evidence as to what opportunities there were for men who were not clerics to judge for themselves of the characters of ecclesiastical persons, and especially of the Religious.

That laymen were commonly well informed as to the doings of the secular clergy has not been doubted, but how far the internal affairs of the religious houses were known to the world outside is less certain. When bishops visited monasteries, as has already been pointed out, great care was taken to exclude laymen and even the secular clergy; and for a monk or canon to reveal the secrets of his house to those outside was a serious offence. We know, too, that the monks were often extremely anxious to prevent reports of scandals concerning their order from spreading. The story of an attempt by the monks of Bury St Edmunds to conceal a serious crime for this reason is recorded on the Patent Rolls, and seems remarkable enough to be worth quoting at some length.

Whereas lately, as the king has learned, a strife arose between Brothers John de Norton, John de Grafton and William de Blundeston, monks of the abbey of Bury St Edmund, by night in the dormitory of the abbey while the other brethren slept, and the said John de Grafton, with a knife called a 'thwytel' suddenly struck John de Norton to the heart in the presence of William, but without his consent, so that he straightway died; and afterwards the abbot and other monks, finding the dead body in the dormitory, totally ignorant of the deed and terrified lest scandal should come on the house, thinking the crime could be secretly concealed and, as it were, put out of mind, in ignorance of the law, buried the body in the cemetery of the monks there without view of the coroner or office of other ministers required in such a case; and afterwards, when the said abbot and convent learned the truth of the matter, the abbot with the assent of the convent had the said John de Grafton and William taken and put them in prison forte et dure (*forti et dura*), as pertains to him by the rule of the order, to undergo the punishment for their delict according to the said rule, in which prison they are detained; the king, in consideration of the innocence of the said abbot and convent and of the fact that they have humbly submitted themselves to the king as ignorant of the said felony, and willing to provide for their excuse for the avoidance of scandals and damages which might happen to them and the house, has pardoned them his suit for the said death and burial, and for this that the prior and convent received the said John and William after the said felony. Moreover, considering that the said felony was done in hot conflict and not of malice aforethought, and that the said John and William have long sustained the peine forte et dure of imprisonment, as the king is informed, he has pardoned them his suit for the said death.[1]

The narrative of this incident is probably based on a petition of the abbot and convent. That a monk had been murdered and his body buried, without having been viewed by the coroner, there is no reason to doubt, but it is hard to believe that the convent were at first so ignorant either of the crime or of the law

[1] *Cal. Pat. Rolls*, 1367–70, p. 186.

in such cases as is here alleged. However this may have been, the important fact is that in spite of all attempts at concealment, the crime could not be kept secret. For some reason, probably because a rumour of it had spread abroad, the monks found it necessary to explain their conduct to the king. Their offence was indeed pardoned, but apparently they had to find six mainpernors for their future good behaviour. The names of the six sureties are given, and it is noteworthy that they were all laymen and secular clerks. The story of the crime must have been known to these men, and it cannot be believed that they would for long keep such a tale to themselves. This is, of course, an exceptional case, both the murder and the conduct of the monks when the corpse was discovered would naturally excite the curiosity of anyone who heard even the vaguest rumour concerning the affair, and for that reason it may have been more difficult to conceal than a more commonplace scandal would have been. There is, however, plenty of evidence to show that misdeeds of all kinds which had been committed by the Religious were well known to their secular neighbours. No surviving records offer clearer or more constant proofs of this fact than the administrative documents with which we have been dealing. In them we see that the local officials, particularly those of the shires, most of whom were country gentry, were constantly brought into contact with the Religious as law breakers. Sheriffs and others were frequently ordered to assist in the capture of apostate monks like the deprived abbot of Bindon. The escheator from time to time took possession of property in the king's name because some religious house had acquired it without licence, or sometimes because the pious work for which it had been granted was not maintained; and numerous country gentlemen were called upon to hear and determine cases of trespass committed by, as well as against, the Religious. Facts that would come to light in the performance of all these duties would be sufficient to show that the standards of the Religious were sometimes no higher than those of their lay neighbours. Still more illuminating were the inquisitions into wastes and the neglect of established works of piety, which accompanied the royal visitations of hospitals and free chapels, and the king's attempts to assist impoverished monasteries. It is important to observe that whenever the crown desired information with regard to a religious house, whether the question concerned the cessation of chantries, the morals of the master and brethren of a hospital, or the alienations of monastic lands, the means taken to procure it were almost invariably the examination of a jury on oath. If the men of the neighbourhood could not have been expected to know more about the internal affairs of ecclesiastical foundations, whether of seculars or regulars, than the ecclesiastical records would lead one to suppose, the summoning of juries would have been of little use. No one, however, seems to have thought a jury unlikely to be able to furnish the desired information, and the jurors were usually ready enough to give evidence with regard to any matter on which they were questioned. Thus the jury which was summoned to give their testimony on an information that Thomas Pipe, the abbot of Stoneleigh, had alienated the lands of his monastery, furnished elaborate details of the grants which he had made, and added that his waste of the abbey's goods was in order to support his concubine, by whom he had more children than there were monks in the monastery.[1]

Alienations of land were, of course, matters that could not well be kept secret, and it might be almost equally impossible to conceal such a scandal as Thomas Pipe's relations with his concubine. It would, therefore, be absurd to argue from such cases as this that all the internal affairs of a monastery were known to those outside. But the evidence seems sufficient to show that the lay neighbours of a religious house were likely to know sufficient to be able to judge for themselves of the character of its inmates. The bishop's visitation is often based on *communis fama*.

The records relating to the assistance of impoverished monasteries, moreover, show that there were a few laymen whose duties gave them exceptional opportunities of acquiring first-hand information as to the affairs of religious houses. These were, of course, the royally appointed custodians. They were sent to assist monasteries which were known to be in distress, very often, as we have seen, through the fault or incompetence of their inmates. The custodians, if they were to render any real service, must have required to be informed of the convent's resources and expenses, and thus the extravagance of the monks,

[1] *Coram Rege*, Hil. 38 Edward III, m. 14; Easter, 38 Edward III, m. 34.

and, often too, the causes which had led to it must have been laid bare before them. Where the impoverishment of a monastery was due only to mismanagement, the commissioners who were sent to assist it might fulfil their functions without losing their respect for the unfortunate Religious. They might even regard the monks' lack of worldly wisdom as, on the whole, to their credit. But what impressions must the custodians have received from a house like Abbotsbury, whose abbot refused to sacrifice his personal comfort and dignity for the good of the house; or like Bindon or Lilleshall, which were distracted by internal dissensions in which armed force was freely used? To hold in reverence such men as the deposed abbot of Bindon must have been impossible for any person of sense who was acquainted with his history, and, as we have seen, there were probably many laymen who would possess personal knowledge of such histories. In fact, the official records of this half-century would furnish plenty of material for the bitterest complaints and the most scathing satires of the time.

Some doubts as to the honesty of ecclesiastical persons, both seculars and regulars, are expressed in the regulations of chantries. Attention has already been drawn to the precautions which several founders thought necessary to ensure the faithful service of their chantries, and one further instance of this may be here cited. On the Close Rolls of 1352, we find an enrolment of an indenture between John de Insula of Rougemont, and the prior and convent of Bolton in Craven, setting forth in some detail the financial arrangements for the chantry which the knight was about to found. It was to consist of six chaplains, two regular and four secular priests, whom the prior and convent were to maintain out of the revenues of the church of Harwood, which John promised to have appropriated to them at his own expense; and until the appropriation could take place, they were to receive forty pounds a year from John's lands. Elaborate details as to the rights of patronage and other matters follow, and then, towards the end of the document, occurs this clause:

and they grant, to make the chantry perpetual, an annuity of 100*l.* to John to be received from certain lands which he shall name, by defeasance, that if the chantry is made and maintained according to the agreement the said annuity shall remain in suspense; and if the chantry cease for a month, unless by destruction of common war or by pestilence, or the land or advowson are recovered and the appropriation undone by judgment..., then the annuity shall remain in force until the chantry is begun again.[1]

That such an agreement should have been devised to ensure the performance of the chantry shows clearly that the good faith of ecclesiastics could not be relied upon implicitly even in a matter which concerned the welfare of souls.

In marked contrast to this anxiety lest the revenues of chantries should be turned to other uses, but probably one of the main causes of misgivings on this subject, was the readiness shown by clerics and laymen alike to misapply other ecclesiastical endowments. No better illustration of this could be found than the record relating to John de Insula's chantry which has just been cited, for from it we learn that while imposing a heavy penalty on the canons in case they neglected the appointed services, he intended to provide for the chantry through the appropriation of a parish church, apparently with no thought as to how the change might affect the parishioners whose tithes were to support this pious work. He even undertook to "use his power, ...that one of the canons of the said house shall be vicar there..., and that his portion shall be made as small as is proper; and by the same manner a secular vicar if there cannot be a canon there".[2]

It would, however, be unfair to regard John de Insula as more selfish in this respect than the majority of his contemporaries, for though throughout the later Middle Ages moralists constantly denounced the system of appropriations of churches, and the conferring of benefices with cure of souls on men who would not be personally responsible for their parishes, the average possessor of an advowson clearly regarded it as mainly a source of profit to himself. In fact, the general attitude towards ecclesiastical patronage in the fourteenth century closely resembled that with which, in the eighteenth century, government patronage was regarded. Reformers might decry the evils of the system, but the average man, especially if one or more advowsons were in his possession, probably saw little need for change.

[1] *Cal. Close Rolls*, 1349–54, pp. 520–1.
[2] *Ibid.* 1349–54, p. 520.

Moreover, even those who perceived the need for reform were forced by the conditions of life to acquiesce in what they knew to be an evil. Thus in the absence of other provision for university teachers, Wycliffe lived at Oxford on the income which he derived from ecclesiastical preferment which he held elsewhere; just as, four centuries later, some men who were eager for parliamentary reform were themselves the representatives of rotten boroughs. No item on the Patent Rolls of our period contains even an implied criticism of the way in which church patronage was habitually used, and in only one instance is disapproval of the appropriation of churches expressed. This occurs in a licence which Helming Leget, a lay official about the court, obtained in 1376 to grant certain specified property "to John Hotot, parson of the church of Fanchirche, London, and his successors, parsons secular of the said church", to support various charges and works of piety,

> provided always that if it happen that the said church at any future time be appropriated to a religious house or college or put in any wise under the cure of any other than under the cure and rule of a parson in secular manner, as it is at present, the premises shall remain to the keepers of the works of the said church for the support and doing of the same works for ever.[1]

But however little respect ecclesiastical persons, as individuals, might command, we meet with no doubts as to the efficacy of the services which they performed. For the very documents which reveal most clearly the existing distrust of the clergy as men owe their existence to the desire to procure those spiritual services which only priests could perform. As has been shown, the founding of masses was, by far, the most popular work of piety, and not only was this so, but the contributors to almost every beneficent enterprise, whether it was the support of the poor in a hospital, the establishment of a college at a university, or the repair of a bridge, were rewarded, and perhaps induced to be liberal, by promises that their souls should be commended in the masses of some priest. We may hope and believe that many persons who sought to further education, or to relieve the poor and the sick, thought more of the immediate objects of their charity than of the spiritual advantages which it was to obtain for

[1] *Cal. Pat. Rolls*, 1374–77, pp. 248–9.

themselves. Yet, through the teaching of the church, which exalted the mass above all other services and charitable works, not only as a spiritual aid to the individual who heard it, but also as conferring benefits on the souls of those on whose behalf it was celebrated, the form, if not the reality, of self-interest appears in the great majority of the charitable gifts of our period.

(2) *The Black Death*

The evidence which these records supply as to the effects of the pestilence has been discussed in the foregoing chapters, and here, therefore, it need be only briefly recapitulated.

The extent to which the monasteries suffered is a question that cannot fairly be answered until many other sources have been examined. But if we are right in assuming that the most serious cases of monastic poverty and disorder were those in which the king intervened, we may infer from the fact that the number of such cases did not increase after the pestilence, that neither the material nor the moral condition of the Religious had been so seriously impaired as has sometimes been supposed. It has often been asserted that the monastic orders fell in popular esteem after the pestilence; and the Patent Rolls contain some evidence which, at first, suggests that this was so, since there was a marked diminution in the number of licences for alienations in mortmain to the Religious.

This may, however, be due only to the general impoverishment of the country, as a result of which many persons could less easily afford to bestow property on the church; and through which, also, the monks' profits derived from their estates were reduced so that the means at their disposal for purchasing additional property would be curtailed. At any rate, it would appear that the monks were not neglected in favour of other ecclesiastics, for grants to all classes of the clergy were fewer, and even chantries were less frequently endowed than they had been before the pestilence.

In comparing the period before and after the plague, there is one change to be noted which affected all types of ecclesiastical foundations. It is the great reduction in the numbers of licences for the appropriation of parish churches. How far this change may be due to the pestilence is uncertain, but whatever may have been its cause, it is, like the contemporary increase in the presentation of ordained priests to parochial livings, an important sign of improvement in the church life of the time.

(3) *Church and State*

Finally, something must be said concerning the relations of the civil and ecclesiastical powers, as depicted in the foregoing studies. They are of particular interest because they are concerned not with what was said and done in great crises when both church and crown were likely to put forth extravagant claims, but with their every-day relations in normal times.

We see that the crown performed a number of functions which one might expect would have been left to the ecclesiastical authorities. Thus, royal officials, with powers similar to those which bishops sometimes gave to the custodians whom they appointed, were sent to assist impoverished monasteries. In a number of collegiate churches and hospitals, moreover, the crown exercised the rights of the official visitor; and, as we have seen, the men who visited these houses on the king's behalf sometimes treated unsuitable members of the foundations with greater severity than they could have expected from a bishop. We see also that the state did not leave the performance of established works of piety to be enforced by ecclesiastical censures only, but that it provided a legal remedy for the founder whose gift was misused, and that it intervened sufficiently often to show that the statute on this subject was not a dead letter. In all these matters the state had little or no temporal advantage to gain, and what was done was largely in the interests of the church itself.

But the state had also to protect itself against the growing power of the church; and one of the most important means by which this was accomplished was the enforcement of the Statute of Mortmain. It may be freely admitted that this statute did not fulfil its avowed object of lessening the number of grants made to the church; to have endeavoured seriously to do this would not only have aroused the hostility of the clergy, but would also have outraged the feelings of the great majority of laymen, since it would have deprived them of one of the most trusted means of providing for their eternal welfare. Men might, and often did, complain of the wealth of the church and of its misuse; and their own financial interests, moreover, would lead them to desire that their tenants should not grant land in mortmain; but probably many of those who, in theory, were most anxious to restrict the church's acquisitions, or even to deprive it of some of the property which it already held, would have desired exceptions to be made in favour of those ecclesiastics whom they themselves wished to endow for their own salvation. It is doubtful, therefore, whether any government had either the power or the will to prevent the granting of land or rent to the church; but the increase of the church's property meant, in the end, the impoverishment both of the immediate overlord and of the crown. In such circumstances, a statute which might tend to lessen the number of alienations in mortmain, by placing difficulties in the way of such grants, and which would give both to the crown and to the overlord a means of deriving some profit from the transaction, might seem the only practicable solution of the difficulties caused by the ever-increasing wealth of the church which the religious feelings of the time would have tolerated.

Whether the influence of the state in ecclesiastical affairs was on the whole a blessing or an evil is a difficult question, and one to which historians would be likely to give different answers according to their views of the proper spheres of clerical and secular authority. But at any rate the degree of control which the state was able to exercise over the affairs of the church was an important factor in the life of the times; and if, as there is every reason to believe, it was maintained throughout the Middle Ages, it must have made the changes which followed the breach with Rome less startling to the ordinary man than they otherwise would have been.

APPENDIX

In the following table, the numbers of licences for alienations in mortmain that were issued year by year are analysed.

In the hope of making the table more useful as an indication of the effects of the Black Death, I have omitted those licences which merely allowed exchanges of property. I have also omitted cancelled licences, if the record shows that the cancellation took place because the licence was not carried out.

Under the heading of friars, I have included only the four orders of Dominicans, Franciscans, Augustinians, and Carmelites, since it seemed better to include the Trinitarian friars and others, whose mode of life resembled that of the regular canons, among the monks and canons. Some thirteen licences on behalf of the Knights of St John have also been included among the licences to the monks and canons. There were also seventeen licences for grants in mortmain to guilds, but since the object of these was almost invariably the support of chaplains, I have included these among the grants made to or on behalf of the secular clergy.

Table of Mortmain Licences

	Monks and regular canons	Nuns	Friars	Hospitals	Secular clergy	University colleges	Total
1327	19	3	1	6	22	2	53
1328	31	1	2	3	33	3	73
1329	28	2	7	9	32	2	80
1330	22	4	5	5	32	—	68
1331	34	4	6	5	36	1	86
1332	30	6	7	4	38	2	87
1333	11	1	3	3	27	—	45
1334	26	2	4	9	35	—	76
1335	33	3	3	4	21	—	64
1336	42	4	6	5	32	—	89
1337	35	1	8	6	33	1	84
1338	31	3	8	1	34	—	77
1339	25	2	1	3	15	—	46
1340	29	4	2	4	28	—	67
1341	18	4	4	6	21	1	54
1342	37	2	2	1	16	—	58
1343	24	1	4	4	26	—	59
1344	34	3	6	5	39	2	89
1345	28	3	3	2	44	—	80
1346	25	2	2	3	24	—	56
1347	21	2	1	4	26	—	54
1348	15	4	3	—	25	2	49
1349	26	4	8	9	41	1	89
1350	30	2	17	4	29	1	83
1351	19	3	6	2	34	1	65
1352	15	2	9	6	33	3	68
1353	17	2	4	2	25	—	50
1354	20	2	3	4	15	1	45
1355	12	1	2	3	16	—	34
1356	14	2	5	1	29	—	51
1357	5	3	2	2	11	—	23
1358	28	3	3	3	23	—	60
1359	20	4	—	3	20	2	49
1360	20	3	—	3	12	—	38
1361	21	6	3	2	31	—	63
1362	25	—	3	3	34	1	66
1363	32	2	3	4	20	1	62
1364	23	5	2	3	20	2	55
1365	24	4	2	4	19	—	53
1366	34	3	—	3	18	1	59
1367	20	2	—	4	7	—	33
1368	15	1	—	2	21	—	39
1369	30	2	2	6	16	—	56
1370	14	4	2	7	15	—	42
1371	14	1	—	3	25	—	43
1372	10	1	3	1	5	—	20
1373	22	2	—	2	18	1	45
1374	13	1	1	5	10	—	30
1375	11	4	2	—	10	—	27
1376	15	3	3	—	19	1	41
1377	11	1	—	2	6	—	20
	1158	134	173	185	1221	32	2903

BIBLIOGRAPHY

PRINTED ORIGINAL SOURCES

Official Records of the State

Calendarium rotularum chartarum (1199–1483) et inquisitionum ad quod damnum (1307–1461) (R.C.). London, 1803.
Calendar of Chancery Warrants preserved in P.R.O., 1244–1326. London, 1927.
Calendar of Close Rolls, Edward I; Edward II; Edward III; Richard II. London, 1892–1927.
Calendar of Fine Rolls. Vols. I–XI. London, 1911–29.
Calendar of Inquisitions, Miscellaneous (Chancery). Vols. I, II. London, 1916.
Calendar of Inquisitions post mortem and other analogous documents. Vols. II–X. London, 1906–21.
Calendar of Patent Rolls, Henry III; Edward I; Edward II; Edward III; Richard II. London, 1891–1916.
Rotuli Parliamentorum. Vol. II. London, 1767.
Statutes of the Realm. Vol. I. London, 1810.
Year Books of Edward II. (Selden Soc.)
Year Books of Edward III. (Rolls Series.)

Ecclesiastic Records

Calendar of entries in the Papal Registers relating to Great Britain and Ireland.
Papal Letters. Vols. I–VI. London, 1893–1904.
Petitions to the Pope. Vol. I. London, 1896.

EPISCOPAL REGISTERS

Bath and Wells
John of Drokensford (1309–29). Ed. Hobhouse, E. (Somerset Record Soc.) London, 1887.
Ralph of Shrewsbury (1329–63). Ed. Holmes, T. S. (Ibid.) London, 1896.
Chichester
Robert Rede (1397–1415). Ed. Deedes, C. 2 parts. (Sussex Record Soc.) Lewes, 1908, 1910.
Coventry and Lichfield
Roger de Norbury (1322–58). Ed. Hobhouse, E. (William Salt Archaeol. Soc., Collections.) Birmingham, 1881.
Robert de Stretton (1358–85). Ed. Wilson, R. A. 2 vols. (Ibid. new series.) London, 1905, 1907.

Durham

Richard of Bury (1338–45). The Register of Richard de Kellawe. Ed. Hardy, T. D. Vol. III (Rolls), 1875; vol. IV (Rolls), 1878.

Exeter

Walter Bronescombe (1257–80) and Peter Quivil (1280–91).
Walter de Stapledon (1307–26). London, 1889, 1892.
John de Grandisson (1327–69). 3 vols. London, 1894, 1899.
Thomas de Brantyngham (1370–94). 2 vols. 1901, 1906.
All edited Hingeston-Randolph, F. C.

Hereford

Thomas of Cantilupe (1275–82). Ed. Griffiths, R. G. and Capes, W. W. London, 1907.
Richard of Swinfield (1283–1317). Ed. Capes, W. W. 1909.
Adam of Orleton (1317–27). Ed. Bannister, A. T. 1908.
Thomas Charlton (1327–44). Ed. Capes, W. W. 1912.
John de Trillek (1344–61). Ed. Parry, J. H. 2 parts. 1910, 1912.
Lewis Charlton (1361–69). Ed. Parry, J. H. 1913.
William Courtenay (1370–75). Ed. Capes, W. W. 1913.
John Gilbert (1375–89). Ed. Parry, J. H. 1913.
Issued jointly by the Cantilupe Society (Hereford) and Canterbury and York Society (London).

London

Ralph Baldock (1304–13); Gilbert Seagrave (1313–16); Richard Newport (1317–18); Stephen Gravesend (1318–38). Ed. Fowler, R. C. (Canterbury and York Soc.) London, 1911.
Simon Sudbury (1362–75). Ed. Fowler, R. C. (Ibid.) 1927.

Rochester

Hamo de Hethe (1319–52). Ed. Johnson, C. (Ibid.) Parts 1, 2, 3, 4. 1914–31.

Winchester

John of Sandale (1316–19) and Rigaud de Asserio (1320–26). Ed. Baigent, F. J. (Hampshire Record Soc.) London, 1897.
William of Wykeham (1366–1404). Ed. Kirby, T. F. (Ibid.) 1896, 1899.

Worcester

Godfrey Giffard (1268–1301). Ed. Willis-Bund, J. W. 2 vols. (Worcester Hist. Soc.) Oxford, 1902.
William de Geynesburgh (1302–7). Ed. Willis-Bund, J. W. (Ibid.) 1907, 1929.
Walter Reynolds (1308–13). Ed. Wilson, R. A. (Ibid.) London, 1927.
Thomas de Cobham (1317–27). Ed. Pearce, J. H. (Ibid.) 1930.
Sede vacante (1301–1435). Ed. Willis-Bund, J. W. (Ibid.) Oxford, 1893–97.

York

William Wickwane (1279–85). Ed. Brown, W. (Surtees Soc.) Durham, 1907.

John de Romeyne (1286–96) and Henry of Newark (1296–99). Ed. Brown, W. (Ibid.) 1914, 1917.

Thomas of Corbridge (1300–4). Ed. Thompson, A. Hamilton. (Ibid.) 1925, 1928.

MISCELLANEOUS

Bird, W. H. B. Calendar of the Manuscripts of the Dean and Chapter of Wells. Vol. I. Historical Manuscripts Commission. 1907.

Clark, A. The English Register of Godstow Nunnery near Oxford. 2 vols. London, 1906, 1911.

Clark, J. Willis. Customs of the Augustinian Canons. Cambridge, 1897.

Coulton, G. G. Visitation of the Archdeaconry of Totnes (1342). E.H.R. XXII (1911), pp. 108 ff.

Crosby, Rev. J. H. List of Incumbents in Cambridgeshire Parishes compiled from Ely Episcopal Registers and other sources (Cambridge University Library, Add. 6380).

Duckett, Sir G. F. Visitations of English Cluniac Foundations. London, 1890.

Foster, C. W. and Thompson, A. Hamilton. The Chantry Certificates for Lincoln and Lincolnshire. Associated Architectural Societies' Reports and Papers. Vols. XXXVI, XXXVII. 1921.

Dugdale, W. Monasticon Anglicanum. Ed. Caley, J., etc. 6 vols. London, 1846.

—— The History of St Paul's Cathedral. Ed. Ellis, H. 1818.

Fowler, G. H. A Digest of the Charters preserved in the Cartulary of the Priory of Dunstable. (Bedford Hist. Record Soc.) 1926.

Fowler, J. T. Memorials of the Church of SS. Peter and Wilfrid, Ripon. 4 vols. Durham, 1882–1908.

Gasquet, F. A. Collectanea Anglo-Premonstratensia. (Camden Soc.) 3 vols. 1904–6.

Goodman, A. W. Chartulary of Winchester Cathedral. Edited in English. Winchester, 1927.

Gray, Arthur. The Priory of Saint Radegund, Cambridge. Cambridge, 1898.

Johnson, John. A Collection of the Laws and Canons of the Church of England. 2 vols. Oxford, 1850–51.

Laurent, Jacques. Cartulaires de Molesme. 2 vols. Paris, 1907.

Leach, A. F. Memorials of Beverley Minster. Durham, 1898.

—— Visitations and Memorials of Southwell Minster. (Camden Soc.) 1921.

Mansi, J. D. Sacrorum Conciliorum Collectio. Vol. XXV. Paris, 1759.

Paris, Dom Julien. Nomasticon Cisterciense. Ed. H. Séjalon. Solesmes, 1892.
Raines, Rev. F. R. History of the Chantries. Vols. I, II. (Chetham Soc.) 1862.
Reynerus, C. Apostolatus Benedictinorum in Anglia. Douai, 1626.
Royce, D. Landboc de Winchelcumba. 2 vols. Exeter, 1892, 1893.
Salter, Rev. H. E. A Cartulary of the Hospital of St John the Baptist. 3 vols. Oxford, 1914, 1915, 1917.
—— Chapters of the Augustinian Canons. (Oxford Hist. Soc. XXIII.) 1922.
Sheppard, J. B. Literae Cantuarienses. 3 vols. (Rolls.) 1887–89.
Spelman, Sir H. Concilia, Decreta, Leges, Constitutiones in re Ecclesiarum orbis Britannici. 2 vols. London, 1639, 1664.
Tanner, T. Notitia Monastica. Cambridge, 1887.
Taxatio Ecclesiastica Angliae et Walliae Auctoritate P. Nicholai IV, *c.* A.D. 1291. London, 1802.
Thompson, A. Hamilton. Visitation of Religious Houses in the diocese of Lincoln. (Canterbury and York Soc. and Lincoln Record Soc.) 2 vols. London, 1915.
—— The Chantry Certificate Rolls for the County of Nottingham. Thoroton Society Transactions. Vols. XV–XVIII. Nottingham, 1912–14.
Valor Ecclesiasticus. Record Commission. 6 vols. 1810–34.
Walbran, J. R. Memorials of Fountains Abbey. (Surtees Soc.) 2 vols. 1878.
Wigram, Rev. S. R. Chartulary of St Frideswide's. 2 vols. Oxford, 1894, 1896.
Wilkins, D. Concilia Magnae Britannicae et Hiberniae. 4 vols. London, 1737.

Municipal and other Local Records

Armitage-Smith, S. John of Gaunt's Register. Vols. I, II. London, 1911.
Bacon, Nathaniel. 1660 Annalls of Ipswyche. Ed. Richardson, W. H. Ipswich, 1884.
Bickley, F. B. The Little Red Book of Bristol. 2 vols. Bristol, 1900.
Ricart, Robert. The Maire of Bristowe is Kalendar by Robert Ricart, Town Clerk of Bristol 18 Edward IV. Ed. Toulmin Smith, Lucy. (Camden Soc.) 1872.
Riley, H. T. Memorials of London and London Life in the thirteenth, fourteenth and fifteenth centuries. London, 1868.
Sharpe, R. R. Calendar of Letter Books of the City of London. Letter Books E, F, G and H (1314–1399). London, 1903–7.
—— Calendar of Wills proved in the Court of Husting. 2 vols. London, 1890.

Stevenson, W. H. Records of the Borough of Nottingham. 1882.
—— Calendar of the Records of the Corporation of Gloucester. 1893.
Studor, Paul. The Oak Book of Southampton. 2 vols. and supp. Southampton, 1910.

CHRONICLES, ETC.

Anonimalle Chronicon, The (1333–81). Ed. Galbraith, V. H. Manchester, 1927.
Baker, Geoffrey le. Chronicon (1303–56). Ed. Thompson, E. M. Oxford, 1889.
Burton, Thomas of. Chronica monasterii de Melsa. Ed. Bond, E. A. Vols. II, III. (Rolls.) 1867–68.
Chronicon abbatiae de Evesham ad annum 1418. Ed. Macray, W. D. (Rolls.) 1863.
Chronicon abbatie de Parco Lude. Ed. Venables, Rev. E. (Lincolnshire Rec. Soc.) 1891.
Chronicon Angliae (1328–88). Ed. Thompson, E. M. (Rolls.) 1874.
Eulogium historiarum sive temporis (to 1366, with continuation to 1413). Ed. Haydon, F. S. Vol. III. (Rolls.) 1863.
Hemingburgh, Walter de. Chronicon (1048–1346). Ed. Hamilton, H. C. Vol. II. London, 1849.
Knighton, Henry. Chronicon. Ed. Lumby, J. R. (Rolls.) 1889.
Loci e Libro Veritatum (Gascoigne). Ed. Rogers, J. E. Thorold. London, 1881.
Murimuth, Adam. Continuatio Chronicorum. Ed. Thompson, E. M. (Rolls.) 1880.
Reading, John of. Chronica Johannis de Reading et Anonymi Cantuariensis, 1346–67. Ed. Tait, J. Manchester, 1914.

MODERN WORKS

Armitage-Smith, S. John of Gaunt. Westminster, 1904.
Arrowsmith, R. S. The Prelude to the Reformation. London, 1923.
Blomefield, F. History of Norfolk. By Parkin, F. B. and C. 11 vols. London, 1805–10.
Bourdillon, A. F. C. The Order of Minoresses in England. British Soc. of Franciscan Studies, vol. XII. Manchester, 1926.
Capes, W. W. The English Church in the fourteenth and fifteenth centuries. London, 1900.
Chadwick, D. Social life in the days of Piers Plowman. Cambridge, 1922.
Cheney, C. R. Episcopal Visitations of Monasteries in the thirteenth century. Manchester, 1931.
Clay, R. M. The Medieval Hospitals of England. London, 1909.
Coulton, G. G. Five Centuries of Religion. Vols. I, II. Cambridge, 1923, 1927.

Coulton, G. G. Some Chapters in the History of Vicarages. History Teachers' Miscellany, vols. III, IV. Cambridge, 1925, 1926.

Cutts, E. L. Parish Priests and their People in the Middle Ages. London, 1914.

Dalton, J. N. The Collegiate Church of St Mary Ottery. Cambridge, 1917.

Deeley, Ann. Papal Provisions and Royal Rights of Patronage in the early fourteenth century. E.H.R. XLIII (1928), pp. 497–527.

Gasquet, F. A. The Black Death of 1348–49. London, 1908.

Graham, Rose. English Ecclesiastical Studies. London, 1929.

—— St Gilbert of Sempringham and the Gilbertines. London, 1901.

—— The Great Schism and the English Monasteries of the Cistercian Order. E.H.R. XLIV (1929), pp. 373–87.

—— The Taxation of Pope Nicholas. E.H.R. XXIII (1908), pp. 434 ff.

Hartridge, R. A. R. A History of Vicarages in the Middle Ages. Cambridge, 1930.

—— Edward I's exercise of the right of presentation to benefices as shown by the Patent Rolls. Cambridge Historical Journal, 1927, pp. 171–7.

Heepe, Johannes. Die Organisation der Altarpfründen an den Pfarrkirchen der Stadt Braunschweig im Mittelalter. Göttingen, 1913.

Hinderwell, T. History and Antiquities of Scarborough. 2nd ed. York, 1811.

Katz, Emma. Mittelalterliche Altarpfründen der Diözese Bremen im Gebiet westlich der Elbe. Bremen, 1926.

Leach, A. F. The Schools of Medieval England. London, 1915.

Little, A. G. The Grey Friars in Oxford. (Oxford Historical Society.) Oxford, 1892.

—— Studies in English Franciscan History. Manchester, 1917.

Maitland, F. W. Roman Canon Law in the Church of England. London, 1898.

Matthaei, Georg. Die Vikariestiftungen der Lüneburger Stadtkirchen im Mittelalter und im Zeitalter der Reformation. Göttingen, 1928.

Mode, P. L. The influence of the Black Death on the English Monasteries. (A Private Edition distributed by the University of Chicago Libraries, 1916.)

Molinier, Auguste. Les Obituaires Français au Moyen Âge. Paris, 1890.

Mollat, G. Les Papes d'Avignon (1305–78). 2nd ed. 1912.

New, C. W. History of the Alien Priories in England to the Confiscation of Henry V. (A Private Edition distributed by the University of Chicago Libraries, 1916.)

Phillimore, Sir R. J. Ecclesiastical Law. 2 vols. London, 1895.

Power, E. E. Medieval English Nunneries, 1275–1535. Cambridge, 1922.

Putnam, B. H. The Enforcement of the Statute of Labourers, 1349–59. New York, 1908.

—— Maximum Wage Laws for Priests after the Black Death, 1348–81. American Historical Review, vol. XXI, pp. 12–32.

Richardson, H. G. The Parish Clergy of the fourteenth and fifteenth centuries. Transactions of the Royal Historical Soc. 3rd series, VI, pp. 89–128.

Rock, D. The Church of Our Fathers. Ed. G. W. Hart and W. H. Frere. London, 1903.

Rogers, J. E. Thorold. A history of Agriculture and Prices in England. Vols. I, II. Oxford, 1866.

Savine, A. R. English Monasteries on the Eve of the Dissolution; in Vinogradoff's, Sir P. G., Oxford Studies in Social and Legal History. Vol. I. Oxford, 1909.

Serjeantson, Rev. R. M. A history of the Church of St Peter, Northampton. Northampton, 1904.

Smith, J. Toulmin. English Gilds. London, 1870.

Snape, R. H. English Monastic Finances. (Cambridge Studies in Medieval Life and Thought.) Cambridge, 1926.

Thompson, A. Hamilton. Pluralism in the Medieval Church, with notes on Pluralists in the Diocese of Lincoln, 1366. (Associated Architectural Societies' Reports and Papers, XXXIII, Lincoln, 1915, pp. 35–73.)

Tout, T. F. Chapters in Medieval Administrative History. Vols. III, IV, V. 1928–30.

—— The English Civil Service in the fourteenth century. Bulletin of the John Rylands Library, III (1916), pp. 185–214.

—— The Political History of England, 1216–1327. London, 1905.

—— The household of the Chancery and its Disintegration. In Essays in History presented to R. L. Poole, pp. 46–85. Oxford, 1927.

Trevelyan, G. M. England in the age of Wycliffe. London, 1899.

Victoria History of the Counties of England. London, 1900 ff.

Watson, Rev. E. W. The Development of Ecclesiastical Organisation and its Financial Basis. Cambridge Medieval History, VI, pp. 528–58.

Welford, R. History of Newcastle and Gateshead. London, 1884.

Westlake, H. F. The Parish Gilds of Medieval England. London, 1919.

Wilkinson, B. The Chancery under Edward III. Manchester, 1929.

INDEX

CAMBRIDGE: PRINTED BY
WALTER LEWIS, M.A.
AT THE UNIVERSITY PRESS